Much love to my grandchildren Sophia,
Milla and Dasha for now and the future…
Grandpa

<u>Other books by John J. Barnes</u>

Retirement: One man's adventures exploring life's final frontier

<u>Barry and Rebecca Forester Adventure Series</u>
        Death in Sentari
        Death in Montevideo
        Death in Hamburg
        Death in LA
        Allen Island
        Death in Dubai

The 2016 insider's guide to

Southern California Desert Gated Communities

<u>Cities</u>:Bermuda Dunes, Cathedral City, Indio, Indian Wells, La Quinta, Palm Desert, Palm Springs, Rancho Mirage , Thermal and Thousand Palms.

<u>High-end</u> <u>gated communities</u>: Andalusia, Big Horn, El Dorado, Griffin Ranch, Hideaway, Madison, Quarry, Toscana, Reserve, Thermal, Thunderbird, Tradition, and Vintage.

<u>Upper-middle communities</u>: Desert Horizons, Indian Ridge, Indian Wells Country Club, Ironwood, La Quinta Resort and Club, The Citrus, Enclave/Enclave Mountain, Haciendas, La Quinta Country Club, Mission Hills Country Club, Morningside, Mountain View, The Palms, PGA West, PGA West Residence Club, PGA Signature, Rancho La Quinta and Tamarisk.

<u>55+ communities</u>: Heritage Palms, Hovnanian Palm Springs and Terra Lago, Ivey Ranch, Palm Desert Greens, Sun City Palm Desert, Sun City Shadow Hills, Suncrest, Trilogy La Quinta, Trilogy Polo Club, and Villa Portofina.

<u>Mid-priced communities</u>: Avondale, Bermuda Dunes, Chaparral, Desert Falls, Indian Springs, The Lakes, Lake Mirage, Monterey, Oasis, Omni Rancho Las Palmas, Outdoor Resort - Indio, Marrakesh, Palm Desert Tennis, Palm Valley, Rancho Mirage Country Club, Shadow Mountain Resort, Silver Sands, Sunrise and Woodhaven.

<u>Bargain communities</u>: Cathedral Canyon, Deep Canyon, Desert Princess, Indian Palms, Mesquite, Outdoor Resort -Palm Springs, Palm Desert Resort.and Portola Country Club.

My thanks to Jim Armstrong for their careful critical reading and suggestions. He's made this book better.

Email me your opinions and suggested changes, additions and any errors you catch. Thanks.

John J. Barnes

jbarnes3609@gmail.com

About this book

You won't be served puff pieces in the pages that follow. You'll get up-to-date, no-holds-bared pros and cons of each individual community listed.

My 'truth' may not be the only truth, but it'll be an improvement over what you'll get on-line from gated community websites.

Their task is to tell you how wonderful they are. Mine is to be as objective as possible. Plus, by example I'll give you the tools to ask the right questions and get the right answers.

There's also the entertainment value inherent in this book. You'll tour some of the most lavish enclaves known to man and discover what separates super rich gated communities from those of the merely rich and everyone else. And that's not all.

If you're a potential buyer, you'll learn the right questions to ask and gain the necessary tools to evaluate gated communities anywhere. I guarantee it.

What 'Gated community' means
If you're looking for gated subdivisions, this book's not for you. I don't list a gated community unless it offers residents an indigenous clubhouse, pool(s), golf, tennis, or similar amenities.

There are exceptions. Thunderbird and Thunderbird Estates, for example, are basically subdivisions; but in the public mind are considered part of Thunderbird Country Club, so that's how they're treated.

Sources

I talked with financial experts and gated community GMs and HOA officials who provided insight I couldn't have gotten otherwise. My sources shall remain anonymous, but you know who you are. I thank you here.

I've checked re-sales on Trulia.com, Realtor.com and Zillow.com. Zillow often shows a property's sales price history going back as far as ten years. Check five or six homes in an individual development on Zillow.com and you'll be able to check if housing prices are rising or declining.

Since I can't live in every community listed in this book, or know all its residents, some of my observations may be considered cursory, anecdotal or second-hand. So visit on your own, compare my 'take' with what realtors and the appropriate websites say and make up your own mind.

Kings and Commoners

Gathering data has been a problem. Any historian will tell you it's easier to write about kings than commoners because so much more is known about kings.

This is true of gated communities. High-end ones with famous members get talked and written about much more than a mid-level community populated by the 'average' well-to-do family.

I've done my best to counter this tendency by keeping reports on the High, Middle, 55+ and Bargain gated enclaves as similar in length as I can.

You, the reader can help. If you have interesting details I can add to a gated community page, let me know. If your info checks out, I'll include it in this book's next edition.

Why more editions? Because believe it or not, a lot happens from year to year, and 2015 was no exception.

In 2015 in the Coachella Valley, one country club closed, a gated community lost its golf course and clubhouse, plus one new high-end and one new upper-middle development launched; but I'm getting ahead of myself.

How This book is organized

Start with the Table of Contents. It will give you a good outline of how the book is organized. You'll note that I've placed each gated community in a category –High-end, Upper Middle, 55+, Mid-priced and Bargain.

As a generality, only the 'super rich' can afford a high-end gated community. The merely rich will gravitate towards an upper-middle gated community. The well-to-do and everyone else will gravitate to 55+, mid-priced and bargain-priced communities.

You may not agree my categorization and placement of gated communities. If so, mail me at jbarnes3609@gmail.com and state your case. If your argument's compelling, I'll change my assessment.

A community's positioning starts with its average-home purchase price; but of equal importance is what a gated community charges monthly for golf dues, Home Owner Association (HOA), maintenance and utility fees.

You may find a condo 'bargain' inside a high-end gated community but realize that when adding $32K annual golf and HOA Fees there's no way in hell you can afford the place.

Privacy concerns
Famous people don't like to be bothered. Many, when buying into a high-end community will have their business manager, attorney or some other person purchase the property in their name. So even if you somehow get a high-end development's membership list, it may not show the names of those who actually live there.

Keep this in mind
Every community described has its own cheering squad. None of the developments I list are 'bad.' It's just that some offer more than others, are newer, or provide their home owners some other advantage.

What I see as a disadvantage (Example: no tennis courts, or no pool) may not be a problem if you or your family wouldn't use these facilities. You may consider their absence an advantage.

What you won't find
Other than architectural detailing or its lack, most gated community photographs look the same. So I've eliminated photos of smiling, contented, well-fed middle-aged people in resort gear chatting on the golf course, or having a candlelit dinner in the club dining room. Go to the community's website for these.

It's okay to skim
You'll find it fun to browse the hi-end communities as well as more modest ones. They all have something to offer or people wouldn't live there.

The Desert area this book covers focuses exclusively on gated communities in Palm Springs, Rancho Mirage, Cathedral City, Bermuda Dunes, Palm Desert, La Quinta, Indian Wells, Thermal, Thousand Palms and Indio, California.

A Confession

I played golf for 17 years but gave it up before moving to the desert, so you won't find me commenting on the merits and drawbacks to various Valley courses. You'll have to research them on your own.

I play a lot of tennis at a variety of clubs around the Valley, so I do have an opinion about tennis facilities, but unless a facility is substandard, and I've yet to run into one, I won't comment.

Finally, my idea of the ideal gated resort community is a place with lots to do, and this bias affects my judgment. You and your family may be seeking quiet and the chance to relax away from daily pressures. If that's you, be aware that if I say a community lacks this facility or that, my criticism may not jibe with your needs or your evaluation.

The accuracy problem

In my mid-thirties, I worked for Michigan Bell Yellow Pages knowing that each year, the second we published a directory, at least 15% of the listings in any of our phone directories would be wrong.

People moved, had their phone service canceled, a house or apartment building was torn down, a business folded, etc.

That's the problem you face while reading this book. Resident associations change rules, increase HOAs, raise golf membership fees, create new membership categories, etc.

Prices change. Differences remain

What you can rely on are the *relative differences* between gated communities. The high-priced ones likely will remain so vis-à-vis the upper middle, middle and bargain-priced developments.

So please don't rely on the specific $ amounts given. Once you single out a few communities for more serious consideration, you can get the latest numbers.

You can approach this book different ways. Read it straight through, use the Table of Contents to find sections that specifically interest you, or go directly to a specific gated community. Now let's get started.

Glossary

Cities: BD= Bermuda Dunes CC= Cathedral City
IW= Indian Wells   LQ= La Quinta
PD= Palm Desert   PS= Palm Springs
IN= Indio   RM= Rancho Mirage
TH- Thermal   TP-   Thousand Palms

The Valley = The Coachella Valley, where all the above- listed
communities are located.

HOA = Home Owners Association.

K = $1,000
M = $1,000,000

Price for a home/condo: Some communities feature both $500K condos and 1.2M freestanding houses. Such a spread   makes creating an average price impossible; so in such situations I've used $750K. This problem predominates in the 'Upper   Middle' category.

HOA prices are averages used when monthly dues differ by size of property or whether the property is a condo or freestanding home.

Golf initiation fees can sometimes be staggered, starting lower for ages 21-35, more for ages 36-45, etc. I always quote the highest fee unless otherwise noted.

Equity memberships allow you to get some of your money back when you leave. Some clubs allow you to pay less if they keep the $ you give them. The figures I list here don't differentiate. I always quote the highest price.

Monthly golf dues also can differ. Again, I always quote the most expensive. They can be less if you're single, under the age of 50, etc.

Contents

Historical and cultural background of desert gated communities:

Glossary, 12
How desert gated communities evolved, 18-20
Desired gated community amenities, 22,23
The dating scene/ cultural inbreeding,
 Crime, bad neighbors,, Pages 24-26
Why a community's age is noteworthy, 26
Why golf courses die, 30
The drought's impact, 32
The shrinking/evolving golf initiation fee, 32
What you need to know about HOA's, 34

Desert Cities reviewed

Bermuda Dunes, 39
Cathedral City, 41
Indian Wells, 42
Indio, 44
La Quinta, 46
Palm Desert, 48
Palm Springs, 50
Rancho Mirage, 52
Thermal, 54
Thousand Palms, 55

High-end gated communities reviewed

Andalusia at Coral Mountain, 60
Big Horn, 62
El Dorado Country Club, 64
Griffin Ranch, 66
Hideaway, 68
Madison Club, 70
The Quarry, 72
Toscana, 74
The Reserve , 76
Thermal, 78
Thunderbird, 80
The Tradition, 82
Vintage Club, 84

Summary, 86

Comparison Chart, 88
Estimated monthly expense, 89

Upper Middle communities reviewed

Desert Horizons, 95
Indian Ridge, 97
Indian Wells Country Club, 99
Ironwood Country Club, 101
La Quinta Resort and Club plus subdivisions 103
    Bajada Estates, 105
    Citrus Club, 106
    Enclave Estates 107
    Enclave Mountain Estates ,108
    La Quinta Fairways, 109
    Haciendas at La Quinta Resort, 110
    Legacy Villas, 111
    Los Estados, 112
    Painted Cove, 113
    Palmilla, 114
    Point Happy, 115
    Santa Rosa Cove, 116
    Spa Villas, 117
    Tennis Villas, 118

Upper Middle communities reviewed—continued

La Quinta Country Club and subdivisions, 119
    Duna La Quinta, 122
    Hidden Canyon, 123
    Lago La Quinta, 124
    Laguna La Paz, 125
    Montero Estates, 126
    Villas, 127
Mission Hills Country Club and subdivisions, 128
    Mission Hills East, 130
    Mission Hills Tennis Villas, 131
    Fairway Estates, 132
    Lakefront I and 11, 133
    Legacy Oakhurst, 134
    Mira Vista, 135
    Stone Ridge, 136
    Haciendas, 137
    Westgate, 137
Morningside Country Club, 138
Mountain View Country Club, 140
The Palms, 142

PGA West and subdivisions, 144
    PGA Greg Norman, 146
    PGA Legends, 146
    Tom Weiskopf, 146
    Jack Nicklaus Private, 146
    Pete Dye Stadium, 146
    Jack Nicklaus Tournament, 146
    Arnold Palmer, 146
    Residence Club, 148
    Montera at Greg Norman, 149
    Signature, 150
Rancho La Quinta, 151
Tamarisk, 153
Summary, 155
    Comparison Chart, 157
    Estimated monthly expense, 158

55+ Communities reviewed

Date Palm Country Club , 164
Heritage Palms, 166
Hovnanian Palm Springs, 168
Hovnanian Terra Lago, 170
Ivey Ranch, 172
Palm Desert Greens, 174
Sun City Palm Desert, 176
Sun City Shadow Hills, 178
Suncrest, 180
Trilogy La Quinta, 182
Trilogy Polo Grounds, 184
Villa Portofino, 186
Summary. 187
Comparison Chart, 191
Estimated monthly housing expense, 192

Mid-priced communities reviewed

Avondale Country Club,196
Bermuda Dunes Country Club, 198
Vibrante, 200
Chaparral Country Club, 201
Desert Falls Country Club, 203
Indian Springs, 205
The Lakes, 207
Lake Mirage Racquet Club, 209
Marrakesh Country Club, 211
Monterey Country Club, 213
Oasis Country Club, 215
Omni Rancho Las Palmas, 217
Outdoor Resort Indio, 219
Palm Desert Tennis Club, 221
Palm Valley Country Club, 223
Rancho Mirage Golf and Country Club, 225
Shadow Mountain Resort, 227
The Springs Country Club, 229
Silver Sands Racquet Club, 231
Sunrise Country Club, 233
Woodhaven Country Club, 234
Summary, 235
Comparison Chart, 237
Estimated monthly expense, 238

Bargain communities reviewed

Cathedral Canyon Country Club, 243
Deep Canyon Tennis Club, 245
Desert Princess Country Club, 247
Indian Palms Country Club, 249
Mesquite Country Club, 251
Outdoor Resort -Palm Springs , 253
  Palm Desert Resort, 255
 Portola Country Club, 257
Summary, 259
        Comparison Chart, 261
        Estimated monthly house expense, 261

Summary and what you must decide before you buy, 264

Alphabetical Listing of Gated Communities, 276

Author's biography, 306

A brief history of California desert gated communities

Movie stars began visiting Palm Springs in the 1930's to relax and play.

In the early 1950's, Clark Gable and others bought houses in the then=unincorporated area of Bermuda Dunes. A country club sprung up there for movie stars and their friends.

Within the next two decades, Mission Hills Country Club and the La Quinta Resort and Club followed. At the latter, you could rent a cottage or a room, golf, swim, play tennis, dance and eat well for a day, a week or longer.

The gated community emerges

In the 1960's and '70s, developers bought land abutting these and other clubs and built gated subdivisions with their own HOA (Home owners Association) dues that were used for landscaping, exterior maintenance and upkeep. Subdivision residents were granted exclusive access to these golf clubs' golf courses and other facilities, but for a price.

In the 1980s, developers such as Bill Bone began building country club, golf course and housing together inside high walls and locked gates. Bone and other developers used several strategies, some more successful than others.

The many-pool condo strategy

The first community concept was to build condos around swimming pools and the golf course.This multi-swimming pool/condo concept was mostly abandoned a decade later.

Too many unused swimming pools meant needless and expensive upkeep. One big pool attached to the clubhouse was cheaper and served as a social gathering place, saved builders money and saved resident HOAs upkeep costs down the road.

Also, in a condo development, the entire community owns the roofs and landscaping. When such a development didn't have fully funded capital reserves, and most didn't, residents were forced to pay one-time assessments of as much as $40K to fix roof, drainage and other problems.

The free-standing home strategy
By the 1990's, developers learned from their mistakes. Builders switched to individual home clusters. The owner would pay for repair of his own new roof, etc. The HOA was off the hook. This meant lower monthly HOA dues, which made a community more attractive to potential buyers.

FOB seeding strategy
Populating high-end communities required its own strategy. Here's how it works. The developer, in many cases the ubiquitous Bill Bone, buys scrub land and looks for a 'seed.'

A 'seed' is a prominent and very rich individual who is given a choice of the best lots, a free lot or other inducement to join the new community.

This strategy assumes the 'seed' will attract other equally rich friends to join him. These followers then become known as FOB, or 'Friends of Bill.' They, too, are given preference.

Once a nucleus is established, the development will become attractive to others who hope to associate with the prominent people in this 'seeded' nucleus.

The turnover strategy

Once a development is built out, meaning all the lots and spec homes are sold, the contractor collects his profits from his sale of build-able lots and spec' houses, turns the development over to its residents and exits, leaving residents with any problems that emerge later.

Reportedly, every time a Monterey Country Club or Palm Valley Country Club home changes hands, developer Bill Bone **receives** a $4K check. If true, this is a nice deal for Bone.

55+ communities arrive

In the early 1990's a third strategy emerged. Del Webb and other developers began building all-in-one communities for empty nesters. To live in one of these communities, at least one of the purchasers had to be at least 55 years old.

These 55+ communities offered indoor and outdoor pools, multiple golf courses, pottery and other craft rooms not even the most expensive country club communities provided, along with 'low' home prices and HOAs private country club communities couldn't match.

Which brings us to now; but before we examine individual communities and the differences that define each, let's first get rid of some misconceptions you may have about desert communities.

Faulty assumptions

(1) The universal realtor cliché 'Location, location, location' applies in the Desert. This is true to an extent. Example: Indian Wells is the Coachella Valley's most prestigious desert address, with more multi-millionaires per capita than its neighbors; but that's as far as it goes.

Much Indian Wells housing stock is old and many homes and gated communities need updating. Buying in Rancho Mirage or La Quinta offers almost as much prestige but arguably newer and thus more attractive residences.

(2) You'll find more and better facilities at the most expensive communities. Wrong. Often, high-end communities lack indoor pools and tracks, craft facilities for painters and potters and other amenities.

Instead, the Desert's most expensive gated communities offer individual houses that may include these amenities, which the owner doesn't have to share with other residents.

(3) Price determines quality. This depends. You can pay $1M+ for a house in a high-end, upper-middle and even in a mid-price development. The individual houses may indeed offer equivalent quality; but the surrounding environment and the type of people you'll associate will differ and such differences will likely determine where you end up buying.

In high-end gated communities, houses are set far apart, meaning you have more privacy than you might in a mid-range community. Plus your neighbors will be super rich and maybe even famous.

(4) Utility costs are comparable for all desert communities. False. Imperial Irrigation, a co-op serving parts of Indio and La Quinta, has rates 20% cheaper than Edison, which serves the rest of the Valley. For larger homes, especially in the summer heat when air-conditioners run 24/7, the price difference can add up.

Gated Community Amenities

There's no general rule for what a gated community should offer, but here's a good starter list:

Clubhouse with library, meeting rooms, crafts rooms, auditoriums and restaurants

Golf course(s), car race tracks, water slides, etc.

Organized social events (dinners/outings/etc.)

Resident-initiated special interest clubs (Photography, poker, opera, wine, etc.)

24-hour manned security

Pro shops (tennis/golf)

Dog park(s)

Indoor and outdoor running and walking tracks/paths

Tennis, bocce ball and pickle ball

Indoor and outdoor swimming pools

Crafts facilities for potters, painters/ others

Professional management

Monthly or quarterly magazine for residents
Spa and massage therapy

Post office

Small general store

Concierge and business services

Children's play ground

Hiking trails

What you should know about golf courses

Most gated communities offer them. Golf courses provide beauty and serenity, which is why people willingly pay extra to live facing them. For people over 50, they also signal 'exclusivity' and 'the good life.' That said, in most developments golf courses run worrisome deficits.

Also troublesome, the sport is losing adherents among the young, and courses are closing all over the country. Some gated communities are considering shutting their courses because they don't have enough paying golfers.

If golf doesn't interest you, many gated communities offer 'cheaper' Social memberships. So keep that in mind.

Also, in this book you'll find gated communities that offer everything but golf and gated communities centered exclusively around tennis and even race car driving.

Miscellaneous

Social Life

During the Coachella Valley's busy season (November through April), even the stuffiest gated communities organize tennis and golf cocktail parties and dinners, wine tastings, tennis, golf, pickle ball and bocce ball tournaments, clinics and lessons, dances, speaker series, concerts, children's days, golf cart parades, hikes, and other events.

Off season, these activities can vanish, except at 55+ communities, which have sufficiently large full-time populations to support such entertainment even during hot summer months.

Gays and lesbians

There's been one failed experiment I'm aware of in Palm Springs where a gay-only retirement community has opened. Sources tell me it's a major failure. It seems gays don't like being segregated any more than other minorities.

At 55+ communities I know about, there are Rainbow clubs that hold potluck dinners, organize hikes and hold monthly meetings at their community's clubhouse. I've yet to hear of complaints from homosexuals or heterosexuals about any of this, suggesting it's a non-issue.

The dating scene

Other than on-line sites such as Match.com and eHarmony.com, men and woman past the age of 50 have lots of places in the Valley to meet.

The 55+ communities have clubs for singles. Other gated communities have evening get-togethers where the entire community mingles. People also meet in the gym, on the golf course or tennis courts or while sharing some other activity.

There's a strong dance subculture in the Valley that makes it possible for dancers to enjoy this activity three and four nights a week in season, moving from private to club to public venues.

Cultural inbreeding

Older communities can be self-selecting. Some may strike you as heavily WASP, Jewish, Italian or whatever. Friends join friends. In some communities, special areas of the country or state may dominate.

Larger communities (Over 1,000 residences) don't usually favor a specific ethnic or religious group. Smaller communities often can. One or two visits may give you a sense of the prevailing culture, but often not. It pays to be blunt and ask.

Crime

I once had a potted plant stolen from my front entryway. A gardener tending the home across the street was the likely culprit but I was never able to prove it.

In larger gated communities, thieves have been known to jump the fence at night and steal TVs and jewelry from houses owned by out-of-state snowbirds. There's relatively little of this. Most communities provide better security than you'll find in most typical middle- or upper-middle-class suburbs.

Nonpayment

Homeowners who don't pay their HOA or golf dues can have liens placed on their homes. They can accumulate fines that build interest as long as they're not paid. Golf, tennis and other privileges can be denied.

If such measures don't solve the problem, responders that allow gated community entrance can be taken away. Community bylaws differ but tend to use these and other prods to get money owed.

Bad neighbors

If your neighbor consistently lets his dog take a dump on your land or the golf course, if he or she doesn't keep shrubbery and grass cut, parks her giant mobile home in front of your house, swears or otherwise abuses you, you can usually file a grievance with your resident Board. This can result in the miscreant being fined and/or having his or her privileges such as golf course use taken away (*See 'Nonpayment' above.*)

I've not heard of residents being voted out of a community, but if you know of such a case, please email me.

Why a community's age is noteworthy

In the desert, regardless of the city or location, 'New' is king. Sure, a 40-year-old, nicely updated estate in Pacific Palisades is preferable to a new one in, say, Tarzana, but in the Desert, 'new' always trumps 'old,' with few exceptions.

Newer homes and communities have the most efficient insulation and double-pane coated windows, which are of utmost importance in the Desert. A growing number also have or offer solar, meaning cheaper electricity.

Newer homes have fresh paint. Wiring for cable and other plug-in devices is up to code. Newer landscaping adds freshness. HOA fees are lower in newer communities. Reserves are funded. Insurance is up to date and adequate.

Older gated developments and their homes often look tired in comparison, which makes these houses harder to sell and causes their prices to drop.

Gated communities built in the 1960's, 1970's and 1980's often lack gyms. They'll have pools scattered throughout a complex rather than a large pool with cabanas for community socializing. They have racquetball instead of pickle ball courts.

Older communities may be 'undercapitalized,' meaning they have 'issues' with sewer systems, common-area and golf-course watering systems, etc. that require special resident assessments to fix. As stated earlier, such assessments are known to exceed $40,000.

With older communities, a large percentage of units will be rentals. Why? Because many of the original owners are old and no longer make the desert trek, or their children live too far away to visit, have inherited the units and rent them because they can't sell or have no desire to use them.

Case in point: Before buying in the Desert, I rented a small condo several blocks from El Paseo in Palm Desert. The community had been built in the 1960's. The owner's children had been trying to sell the unit for eight years without success.

After finally buying a house, I continued driving by that condo weekly for several years on the way to tennis matches. Once or twice I saw a renter. The rest of the time the condo sat empty, its owners paying the monthly HOA, utilities and the occasional assessment, the one two years prior costing $15K for new fencing and pool resurfacing. So beware! In the desert, 'new' almost always trumps 'old' and for good reason.

Newsworthy
for 2016

New Additions

Since last year's edition of this book we've added 15 new gated Communities:

In Bermuda Dunes, Vivante

In Cathedral City, Portola Country Club

In Indio, Outdoor Resort-Indio

In Thousand Palms —Ivey Ranch

In La Quinta: Bajada Estates, Griffin Ranch,
Los Estates, Palmilla, Painted Cove,
Point Happy Estates, Thermal Club,
PGA West Residence Club, and
PGA West Signature

In Palm Springs, Outdoor Resort—Palm Springs

In Rancho Mirage, Omni Rancho Las Palmas

Ivey Ranch, Portola, Rancho Las Palmas and Residence Club have been around. We unintentionally overlooked them last year *(Sorry, Ivey Ranch, Omni, Portola and Residence.)*.

The Year of the car

The Thermal Club in La Quinta replaces the traditional golf course with a race car circuit for rich people who own fast cars and seek a community to store, service and race them.

Also car-centric, Big Horn has added 'the Vault' so its residents can store their exotic cars there. Is this the start of a trend?

Corporations as partners

The La Quinta Resort and Club is managed by the Hilton Corporation, Rancho Las Palmas is managed by international hotel and resort corporation (Omni).

Both Omni and Hilton funnel in paying vacationers into their gated desert communities for days and weeks at a time, which helps defray their communities' restaurant and golf course costs.

At The Thermal Club, BMW's heavy participation helps defray this community's on-going operating costs.

BMW aside, the negative effect of corporate involvement by hotel chains is lots of rentals and transients that destroy a community's inner cohesiveness and 'feel.' Also, corporate involvement does not ipso facto guarantee financial solvency.

The La Quinta Resort and Club has gone bankrupt more than once. Omni bought Rancho Las Palmas after the previous corporate owner failed, so presumably 'deep-pocketed' corporate ownership doesn't guarantee continued success.

Why two golf courses died

In 2013, the last year for which data is available, 157 eighteen-hole golf courses in the United States folded   and fourteen opened. We can assume this trend will continue. Why is this happening?

Millennials aren't taking up golf. It's seen as too expensive relative to other choices and takes too much time. Conclusion: Well-to-do senior golfers are dying off and not replaced.

Santa Rosa Golf Club in Palm Desert is an example of such forces in action. Santa Rosa is not a gated community, meaning it can't rely on 'captive' homeowners as customers but must consistently generate new members from elsewhere.

Also, Santa Rosa Golf Club's members didn't own their golf course and clubhouse. A developer did. The aging and declining membership tried to buy the land and club from this developer but couldn't afford the mortgage payments, went into default in 2014 and the country club died.

According to the report in the <u>Desert Sun</u>, the developer plans to develop a retirement community on the now shuttered land.

The Rancho Mirage Country Club's golf suffered a similar fate. Its membership also didn't own its golf course. Once again, a developer did.

One gated-community GM told me in confidence that she believed it takes a minimum of "around 800" homes to support a gated community's golf course. Rancho Mirage Country Club has only 256 homeowners.

This suggest that even if a gated community with fewer than 800 members <u>does</u> own its own golf course, the need to keep increasing golf-initiation and monthly fees may eventually reach a tipping point.

Excepting clubs whose rosters are dotted with billionaire members, costs eventually will outrun a membership's desire or ability to pay them, membership numbers will shrink and the club will sell its land to a developer and hope for the best.

Most 55+ communities with 2,000 homes likely survive. At Sun City Shadow Hills, for instance, the golf course costs each member only $17 monthly out of its HOA of $217 per month.

In comparison, forget about high-end golf course developments, at mid-priced The Lakes Country Club HOA/golf dues have reached $1,634 monthly.

How much higher can mid-priced monthly fees rise before memberships in these communities decide to 'cash in their chips' and shut down their clubs?

What can be done?

Clubs with two courses can shut down one of them. Playing days can be curtailed. Worse case, the golf operation can be 'mothballed' until solutions are found.

The Drought

California's water shortage intensified in 2015. Depending on the area, state government mandated case-by-case water-usage reductions from 25% to 36% for businesses and individuals.

The Coachella Valley is home to one of the highest concentrations of golf courses in the world; and each course requires prodigious amounts of water to maintain a vibrant green appearance.

Our Valley's golf courses get water in a variety of ways. Some courses, especially those in La Quinta take water directly from the Colorado River via canal. Others pump water from underground aquifers. Still others recycle their water, drawing from the aquifer to replace what evaporates.

The Coachella Valley generates only an average of 5.5" of rain annually. Valley residents until recently used three times as much water as the average Californian for themselves and for more than 120 courses, a giant Palm Springs water park and thousands of area swimming pools and fountains.

To reduce water use, many homeowners and gated communities are converting some of their land to desertscape. Others are installing recycled water systems, and still others are watering less, leaving close-cropped brown spaces where grass once grew.

When possible, I've asked communities to tell me what they've done to conserve water and have passed on what they've told me to you. You'll find this information in individual community write-ups.

The shrinking/evolving golf membership fee

Equity memberships give the purchaser shares in the golf course and clubhouse. When it comes time to sell their shares, members can, based on varying sets of conditions, sell their shares back to the community or its developer for what they paid.

In some but not all circumstances. Departing members have sold their shares for more than they originally paid, but anecdotal evidence suggests this is becoming less possible. Here's why.

In the past decade, both PGA West and the La Quinta Resort and Club have gone bankrupt. Some members who contracted to sell their equity shares back to the developer still wait for their money, or they've been offered cents on the dollar or partial payment only.

To counter this worry, many golf clubs now offer non-equity memberships at a reduced rate. You give them the initiation fee and that's it. You're out the money but you don't have to worry about never being paid back.

To compensate, many of these same clubs are raising monthly golf dues, expecting to get their lost revenue back over time.

Another problem with equity memberships: You can sell your house and not be able to sell your membership. Maybe the purchaser of your home doesn't play golf. Maybe he/she takes out a cheaper social membership instead.

Departed home sellers finding themselves in this predicament often refuse to pay monthly dues. When their membership finally sells, they get what's left after their delinquent dues are deleted.

Some clubs or their developers put your name on a list. When a new homeowner buys into the gated community, he/she buys from the first name on the list. In some high end communities, where the list is long, you may wait years to sell your equity membership.

One more problem with equity memberships:Once you pay the money, you're saddled with monthly golf dues, and these seldom if ever decrease. Figure on them rising 3-7% a year.

Buyers consider 'total price,' and that includes HOA and golf membership. Before you know it, the dues rise to the point they force down the price when you sell your house. (The Lakes is a classic example of this.)

Worst deal of all: Clubs where the developer retains control of the golf course and clubhouse give you zero control of your investment. (Rancho La Quinta is a good example.)

If the developer for any reason decides to sell or re-purpose the land, the gated community's chief assets (golf course and clubhouse) disappear.

This happened in 2015 at Rancho Mirage Country Club. Its members were left with an ordinary gated subdivision facing an abandoned golf course with the value of their home immediately dropping as much as 40%.

An HOA primer

As stated, HOA monthly costs in most Coachella gated communities can be expected to rise 3-7% each year.

As a general rule, the older the community, the higher the HOA, which means if you're living in a community 15 or more years old, you could be paying three times as much as someone in a newer community for basically the same sized home, services and amenities. Here's why.

Older communities have stuff that's started breaking. Sewer systems, golf course watering systems, roads, swimming pools and sidewalks either need repair or replacing.

Advice: Don't buy in any gated community whose reserves aren't at least 65% funded. *Your realtor should advise you on this. If he or she doesn't, then you've got yourself a bad realtor.*

Advice: Check to see if any one-time member assessments in addition to normal HOA fees have been assessed in the past five years. If there have been such assessments, you've been warned.

Advice: Other factors being equal, if you have a choice between a community with free-standing homes or one with condos, chose the community with free-standing homes. Your risk of dreaded one-time assessments won't go away, but your risk will be less.

Advice: Once one gated community falls in a trap and raises its HOA rates, the managements of similar communities are tempted to do the same, justifying to residents that they are being assessed in line with members of competing clubs.

How can you know if this has happened to a gated community you're interested in? You can't in most cases.

One protection you should exercise: Avoid communities that self manage –unless the community has hired a professional manager. Why?

Most gated communities don't always have members with the requisite financial and management experience   or knowledge of the appropriate state and federal laws. Plus people move, die or stop volunteering. Continuity is lost along with background knowledge and expertise.

Also, self-managed communities must self-insure, thus risking lawsuits and expenses the community may be unable to pay.

The Canadian Dollar

As 2015 neared its end, Canadians began putting their Valley homes on the market to cash in on a 30% premium for the American dollar over the Canadian dollar. At the same time, fewer Canadians could afford second homes in the California desert. The result: Many more homes on the market than usual, which has resulted in lower prices. Recently, the difference between the purchasing power of the American versus the Canadian dollar has narrowed. Once approximate parity resumes, home prices and purchases should rise again.

Summing Up

(1) Avoid gated communities whose members don't own their own course and clubhouse.

(2) Avoid gated communities who self-manage, unless they've hired a professional manager..

(3) Watch for for 'age creep.' It can cause declining memberships and future financial problems. Go to the gym. Walk around the clubhouse and other facilities and form your conclusions.

(4) Avoid equity memberships

(5) Consider the Valley's 55+communities. They generally generally provide more facilities than ever the the high-end communities (e.g., indoor pools), keep monthly HOA costs low, don't charge a golf initiation fee or monthly dues, and have well funded financial reserves.

.

Desert Cities

Some history: As mentioned earlier, in the 1950s, movie stars flocked to Palm Springs. This attracted others. In the 1980's, the people movement into the Coachella Valley picked up but didn't stay hunkered around Palm Springs.

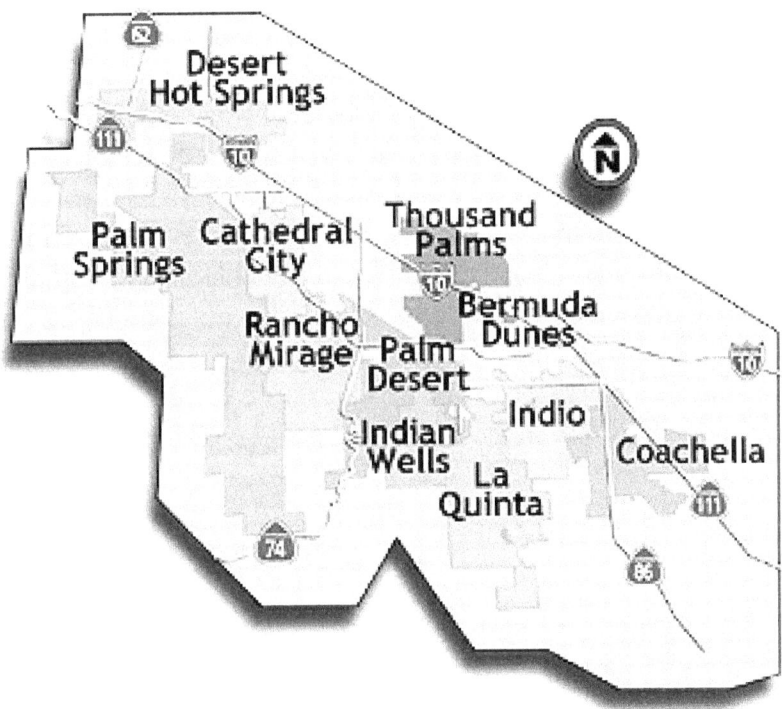

New retail and housing began seeking 'greener pastures' to the west, almost all growth taking place inside the Route Ten and Route 111 corridor.

Development moved into and through Cathedral City to Rancho Mirage, Palm Desert, La Quinta, and most recently into Indio's outskirts.

How does this westward migration of people, homes and retail affect any home choice you might make? Well, if you seek 'newness,' you'll find that the oldest communities in Palm Springs and Cathedral City, the newest in La Quinta and Indio. You'll have to decide for yourself if this makes a difference.

Traffic moves quickly in the Coachella Valley. All its desert communities are a 30-minute drive or less from each other.

Still, it never hurts to understand what each community does and doesn't provide. Each has its distinct personality.

If you find a gated community you like, go for it. In my opinion, the city it's in shouldn't be the decider, but my opinion means little. You're the one who's putting out the money.

On the following pages you'll find brief descriptions of the seven cities that support the gated resort communities we'll critique.

BERMUDA DUNES

I've finally figured out where Bermuda Dunes is. Travel Adams Road or Washington Boulevard near Freeway 10 and tucked between La Quinta and Indio is the Bermuda Dunes Golf Club. It serves as sort of a town center. There's no city hall. Basically, other than the Bermuda Dunes Golf Club, what you'll find are individual homes or small home clusters intermixed with dusty scrub, wholesale nurseries, some small businesses on Adams and Washington and that's it. Wikipedia defines Bermuda Dunes as a 2.9-square-mile 'census-designated place' (CDP). You'd think an abutting city like Indio or Palm Desert would annex Bermuda Dunes, but this hasn't happened. In short, there's 'no there there,' unless you count the country club as 'there.' I suspect that if it weren't for the Bermuda Dunes Country Club, there'd be no Bermuda Dunes, period.

CATHEDRAL CITY

This book doesn't spend much time here because Cathedral City has only three gated communities listed, and two of them are old and comprised of mostly rental units. Cathedral City used to have an Imax theater, but despite being subsidized by the city, it went bankrupt.

Cathedral City has an Elks Club and a large auto mall where you can buy Hyundais, Fords, Mazdas, Cadillacs, Buicks, Volvos, Kias, Volkswagens and Lexuses. It has a Cineplex. Someone told me it has one pretty good restaurant. My source has since moved away. No one I ask knows of any such restaurant.

INDIAN WELLS

This may arguably be not only the most prestigious but the best of all the desert cities to live in. Palm Desert's El Paseo high-end shopping center and restaurants are five minutes away. Your resident card gets you free use of the Hyatt Regency Indian Wells Resort & Spa/fitness center. You get 20% discount on meals at

nts at all Indian Wells resorts. Residents have their own IW Club, which recently underwent a multi-million dollar renovation. The Indian Wells Tennis Garden is the world's second-largest tennis stadium. The BNP Paribas Open (the fifth-most attended professional tennis tournament in the world) is held there. The local Hyatt Regency, Indian Wells Resort Hotel, Miramonte Resort & Spa, and Renaissance Esmeralda Resort are luxury oases within the City. Indian Wells' Desert Town Hall speaker series and World Affairs Council of the Desert bring the world's foremost leaders each winter to speak to sold-out audiences.

Two years ago, Indian Wells spent millions planting tall palms and flowers on the meridians ofHighway 111, which bisects the city. Indian Wells enjoys the luxury of a $30-million General Fund reserve 'just in case.' Population includes 5,000 full-time homeowners and renters supplemented by another 4,000 seasonal residents. It's home to the Vintage Club, with arguably the Desert's most distinguished membership. Other gated communities include the Eldorado Country Club, The Indian Wells Country Club, Desert Horizons Country Club and Toscana.

INDIO

This city is famous for its Coachella music festivals located at Indio's Empire Polo Club during two, three-day April weekends each year. The week following the rockers and rappers you can

hear the country's most popular country acts and entertainers at the Stagecoach Music Festival. The February Indio Date Festival is held in honor of the region's top date producer and is part of the annual County Fair that features camel races. The Fair dates (pun intended) from 1921. I went one year. It was sort of fun. There's also a tamale festival. I've not been.

Indio's polo fields might tempt you to think that Indio is filled with rich people.The opposite is true. Of all the desert cities we cover, it's home to some of the poorest families and individuals. Indio has some terrific Mexican restaurants, but the downtown is no beauty, filled with   the usual fast food emporiums, a county jail,

Booth at Indio's annual Date Festival.

check cashing and bail-bond places. Indio residents enjoy the frequent sight of balloonists at dawn and dusk, sometimes four or five balloons at a time. They rise from the polo fields and settle there after they're done. Gated communities include 55+ developments Sun City Shadow Hills, Heritage Palms, Hovnanian Four Seasons Terra Lago, and Trilolgy at the Polo Club.

LA QUINTA

This part of the Coachella Valley feels more like a clustering of huge gated communities than a city developer did build 'La Quinta Old Town,' but it doesn't look old or town-like. It's basically no more than a modestly successful retail strip. On the plus side, La Quinta has more high-end gated golf communities than any nearby town. The Reserve, Hideaway, Madison Club, huge PGA West development, La Quinta Resort and Club and others give the area lots of golf courses (25) plus thousands of well-to-do visitors from November through April every year. The city is anchored by the La

La Quinta's Civic Center campus.

Quinta Resort & Club, founded in 1926. Go on the website to research La Quinta's 'history' and you'll realize there isn't any. It was just empty land until the La Quinta Resort and Club was built. The new city and its gated communities incorporated around this resort.The La Quinta Arts Festival in March is billed as the U.S.A.'s largest. Maybe so, but that just means there's more predictable professional art, most of which you've seen at such festivals since you started going to them. The city reports it has 14,881 property owners, many of them part-time, averaging $93,091 per household, plus 11 parks. I've hiked miles of biking and hiking trails in these parks and recommend them.

PALM DESERT

This city's crown jewel is El Paseo, a street lined with famous sculptors' works, an eclectic restaurant mix, Saks, Brooks Brothers, an Apple store and lots of art galleries, chi chi clothing and jewelry emporiums. Up Portola Avenue waits the Living Desert, a wonderful place to take children with its African animals prowling and noshing in the open. You literally walk or ride by them on a miniature train on your way through this zoo. Then there's the McCallum Theater, which operates during Season with over-the-hill performers but occasionally surprises you with somebody contemporary and good.

Palm Desert's El Paseo Boulevard

Westfield Mall and other shopping centers line Route 111 signifying that Palm Desert is indeed the area's shopping ground zero. In addition, you'll find doctors' offices and a lot of middle and upper-middle class housing running from $300,000 to $1 million+, to include the following gated communities described in this book:

Avondale Country Club
Desert Falls Country Club
Oasis Country Club
Palm Desert Resort
Portola Palms
Shadow Mountain
Sun City Palm Desert

Deep Canyon Tennis Club
Indian RidgeThe Lakes
Palm Desert Green
Palm Valley
The Reserve
Silver Sands
Villa Portafino

If the southern California desert and Coachella Valley had a capitol, Palm Desert would be it.

PALM SPRINGS

Go here to have fun. The Palm Springs downtown when I first arrived in the Desert seven years ago looked as if it were on its last legs, to include empty storefronts and a big empty auto dealership on its outskirts. Since then the city's undergone a renaissance, to

Palm Springs' iconic windmills seen on Route 10 as you approach and leave the city.

include hip young hotels like the Ace, which doesn't have great food or lodging but understands what young people without a lot of money want and provides it. Then there's the Riviera, more upscale done funky Frank-Sinatra-era deco, where you can get a good meal while looking out upon almost naked young bodies frolicking by the huge pool. Outside town, there's a tram to take you literally up into another eco system with Douglas firs instead of Palms and temperatures 20 degrees cooler than on the desert floor.

It seems there's a biker, 50's-modern, gay or other festival happening every week in Palm Springs. There's a Hard Rock Café and even a museum (It's got a branch in Palm Desert), and although there's nothing special about it, it holds parties and is a fun place to browse the art. The downtown still has a touristy, honky tonk vibe but street life has improved. Lulu's allows you to sit outside as if you were in Paris and watch the bizarre foot traffic. A heavy gay element enlivens the mix. Hotels are cheap, many under $100 a night. The most luxurious, the Parker, maybe a mile from the downtown, has so-so overpriced food but cottages and a big swimming pool and glades where you can walk and find peace. There are some beautiful homes within blocks of downtown Palm Springs and in the mountains behind, many of these homes costing multiple millions.

Palm Springs is famous for mid-century architecture.

RANCHO MIRAGE

This city sprawls between Palm Springs and Palm Desert and resembles La Quinta. That's because it, too, is filled with gated communities and subdivisions without a definable 'there' there, unless you consider The River Mall 'there.' The River is a fun mall with a big Cineplex, fountains, and lots of mid-range retail and restaurants. Seventeen thousand people live in Rancho Mirage's five-square-mile area year around. The Ritz-Carlton Rancho Mirage, after a bankruptcy and lots of tax rebates, has finally opened on a bluff overlooking empty scrub, housing and retail on Route 111. The city has a nice contemporary library on Route 111 where you can hear guest speakers and check out a

Rancho Mirage's new library on Route 111.

book, DVD or whatever's being checked out these days. Mission Hills Country Club,a huge gated community that contains smaller gated communities within, holds several golf tournaments. Then there's the 200-acre 25,000-square foot Sunnylands, the Walter Annenberg Estate, where presidents, to include Barack Obama have stayed. Sunnylands' gardens are open to the public. Rancho Mirage's attractiveness is not obvious at first glance. It's mostly flat with a scattering of random gated communities; but such surface observations can be deceptive. Most Rancho Mirage residents live close to main artery 111 with its many shops and restaurants. Eisenhower Medical Center on Bob Hope, arguably the area's best medical facility, sits within Rancho Mirage's boundaries. Hundreds of stand-alone homes in Rancho Mirage sell for the multi-millions, and there's a lot of open land available.

"Sunnylands," or the Annenberg estate has been the meeting place of U.S. presidents and may be Rancho Mirage's most famous attraction. You need a reservation to visit its gardens.

President Obama, after several enjoyable vacation weeks here is reportedly considering this city as his winter retreat once he leaves office.

THERMAL

Thermal rests 25 miles southeast of Palm Springs and 9.5 miles north of the Salton Sea. This unincorporated, census-designated place is not a town, township or anything else. It's included

because The Thermal Club resides here. You get there by traveling the 10 Freeway from LA or Palm Springs until heading east on Route 86. The Jackie Cochran-Desert Cities Airport is nearby and the Union Pacific Railroad has a line that runs through the area. The 2010 Census reports 2,865 people living in Thermal. I've not visited but promise to do so prior to publishing the next edition of this book. By then, the Thermal Club track and supporting facilities should be almost completed with residents occupying some of the homes.

THOUSAND PALMS

Like Bermuda Dunes, Thousand Palms is a 'census-designated' community, meaning you won't find a designated retail strip with a police station, retail stores, gas stations and restaurants. As an area without a core it exists mostly as empty land visible when heading west to Los Angeles on the 10 Freeway. As you pass Palm Desert and Rancho Mirage on your left, on you'll right you'll be looking at Thousand Palms. Per the 2010 Census, this area's population numbered 7,715 with 2,849 households. The Ivey Ranch Country Club, a 55+ development, also can be found there.

Hi-End
Gated Communities

High-end gated community homes are typically priced between $750,000 and $20,000,000

A select few of the following high-end developments are known for being particular about whom they accept. There's a persistent rumor that a certain California U.S. senator was refused admittance by several of these high-end gated communities.

Also, some of these same communities aren't partial to actors and actresses, believing they attract too much attention from the 'wrong' kinds of people.

Let's assume you are rich as Croesus but not acceptable to two or three of the gated communities listed. Not to worry.

Most of the others (although they won't admit it) are eager for members. If your bank balance and financial backup pass muster, you're in.

This may not satisfy you. Groucho Marx once reputedly said he wouldn't want to join any country club that would have him.

Because HOA's and golf dues can run as high as $32K annually and golf initiation fees as high as $350K, your net worth should be in the many millions before even thinking about joining the most 'selective' gated communities.

Unlike 55+ communities, in which 50% of residents stay all year, high-end places empty from May through October and heir restaurants, spas and other services close.

If you live in such a community year around, this won't be a problem if your home is close to supermarkets, barbershops, hair salons, etc. Small communities (less than 500 homes) that aren't close can begin to feel lonely and isolated in late Spring, Summer and Fall.

Many communities reported on here tend to draw from certain cities or counties. They also tend to attract new homeowners who resemble residents already there.

The author has made every effort to include the latest and most accurate data, but the some clubs will change their HOA and other fees after this book's publication.

In all instances, HOA, dues and other $ costs are for 2016. If you spot an error or know of an update, email me at jbarnes3609@gmail.com

Andalusia at Coral Mountain

Avenue 58 at Madison

La Quinta, CA 922

(760) 777-1000

andalusiaatcoralmountain.com

This south La Quinta development opened in 2005 and currently has 170 home owners whose properties range in price from $900K to $2M with 730 lots still looking   for buyers. Two private golf courses are built and in use. The monthly HOA charge is $670,   up $25 from last year. To play golf, a $39.5K non-refundable membership is required with monthly dues $1,100. Nine lakes fill the desert scape and golf course. A 'trial' one-year golf membership is available for $15.5K. Lots of picturesque lakes, streams, rocks and rills make Andalusia a pleasant place to walk. Amenities include a fitness center, enter, nine night-lit tennis courts, golf and tennis pro shops, a 25-meter pool with spa and children's wading pool plus spacious sun decks, but, oddly, no pickle ball courts. There are two restaurants and an actual French chef in residence with home delivery of meals available, a personal concierge to do grocery shopping, floral arrangements, custom cakes, dry cleaning, car rentals, restaurant reservations, house sitting, delivery acceptance, errand running and dog walking. Nice! Opening this year—a new 15,000-square-foot clubhouse with golf pro shop, admin offices and spa services. Members also can play at Rancho La Quinta's two courses located off Washington Ave, which is owned by the same developer, who owns the golf course and clubhouse, which could become a problem if the developer goes bankrupt or decides to use the land it owns for other than a golf course.

Big Horn

255 Palowet Drive

Palm Desert, Ca 92260

(760) 341-4653

This community (established 1992) equals Indian Wells' renown Vintage Club in its ability to attract buyers from the same small pool of super rich business icons. The Vintage is known for its privacy and penchant for turning away Hollywood people. Big Horn brashly advertises itself on late-night television. Its members have contributed over $11 million to support Eisenhower's Radiation Oncology center, $1.6M for Hurricane Katrina victims, $1.6M for breast cancer and $1.5 million for Wounded Warriors. The community's 570 homes sit 1,000 feet above the valley floor.

homes sit 1,000 feet above the valley floor. Reportedly, members get together at the end of the year and write checks to pay for restaurant or golf course deficits. Big Horn recently added a children's playground. For 2016, it has debuted 'the Vault,' an adult playground where members can store exotic cars and have a drink. There are 60 car slots available. An equity membership costs $250K with $27.5K annual dues. A non-equity social membership costs $100K with $16K annual dues. HOA dues run $775 monthly. House prices average$1,750,000.

El Dorado Country Club

46000 East Eldorado Drive
Indian Wells, CA 92210
(760) 346-8081

Established in the late 1950's, El Dorado keeps satisfying
residents while staying 'under the radar.' This may be the only
Valley gated community that has no homes facing directly on its
two 18-hole courses, each course reportedly short by modern
standards but 'challenging.' You'll find few homes for sale. Lots
of glass and 'Bauhaus style' designs characterize Eldorado estates.
Residents tend to stay many years, which is not the norm
elsewhere. The 2015-2016 activities calendar is filled with
Bridge, Mah Jong, bocce ball and other sedentary activities that
suggest an older crowd: but El Dorado does field a tennis team
that conducts inter-club matches with Toscana, Rancho la Quinta,
Tamarisk, etc., so not everyone is sedentary. Formal attire is
required for Friday and Saturday night dining and private
parties. No tank tops allowed.

El Dorado entry gate.

President Dwight Eisenhower was a resident here. Free-standing homes go for as much as $7 to $10 million but most fall in the $1.5M to $5M range. Condos are a different matter. In 2014, I found a 2,000+ square-foot, updated condo built in 1957 listed for $750K that possibly sold for less. Its monthly HOA was

$1,381 plus a second general fee paid semi-annually of $2,930. If you spec out the club's real estate listings you'll find HOAs all over the place, many as low as $5K a year to include cable. 'Cottage' HOA's are a standard $1.5K annually. A golf initiation costs $150K with $25K   annual dues. A Social membership costs $30K plus $10.5K annually. An on-site realtor told me there were approximately 400 homes within the gates. I remarked that that I couldn't find the actual number anywhere and she said, "Yes, we don't like publicity. We play everything 'close to the vest' here."

Griffin Ranch

54-835 Damascus Drive

La Quinta, CA 92253

(760) 501-2960

Griffinranchlaquinta.com

Looking for a high-end gated community with brand new homes but don't want to bother with a golf course? Griffin Ranch may be for you. Its 240 acres were purchased by entertainer Merv' Griffin 30 years ago. He built his own lavish estate there and envisioned an equestrian club for the premises and opened it in 2007, but the recession and his demise that same year stopped everything.

National homebuilder Lennar bought the property in 2013, built a club house in 2014 plus 11 spec houses, and Griffin Ranch was back in business. There will be 221 homes at build-out, a clubhouse with lounge/bar, splash pool for kids, big pool for grownups, caterer's kitchen adjacent to a convention room for 200 guests, tennis courts, putting green, fenced dog park and community barbecue area. The grounds feature rustic split-rail wood fences, tree-lined streets and paver walkways.There are two collections, the Belmont, which range from $820K to $1.028M with 2,967 to 3,771 square feet, and The Pimlico Collection priced from $1.081M to $1.195M with 4,036 to 4,882SF. Many of these homes have three-bay garages and outdoor fireplaces with courtyard lounge areas and pools. The development is adjacent to PGA West and its golf facilities. You can buy a membership there if you want to play golf. There are

he fitness center at Griffin Ranch.

oddities. Like no restaurant or resident French chef available, and five of the homes can be rented, one for either $341 or $241 per night (I saw different prices on two rental sites). Merv' Griffin's original estate also can be rented for $5,339K per night. It sleeps 20, with 13 bedrooms and 'guest pods' scattered throughout its environs. For home owners, the HOA is $650 monthly.

The Hideaway

80-440 Hideaway Club Court
La Quinta, CA 9225
(760) 777-7400

This gated community started selling homes and lots in 2002 and occupies an attractive multi-level piece of property set against a mountain range near the La Quinta 'Old Town' retail area. The houses are huge and 'hacienda' style with enclosed courtyards hidden from the street. Empty but grassed, mowed and watered lots sit between properties, each a half acre or more. At build-out there will be only 440 homes. You buy 'by invitation only,' which means it helps to have a 'clean' professional and personal reputation. A smaller group of 'bungalows' averaging less than 3,000SF is located near the clubhouse. At highest elevation are 'California Village' homes. Monthly HOA's average $600 for custom homes and $965 for bungalows, this higher figure including all outside and some inside maintenance. Lots are said to sell from $300K to $1M, but one of the community's newsletters said the average lot transaction price is $500,000 to $600,000. (To add smoke to the fire, just recently I heard a lot was available for 175K, but this is hearsay.) A golf membership costs $200K, golf dues $2,175 monthly, up $150 from last year, and a Social Fitness

membership $27.5K. Judging by realtor ads in the local *Desert Sun*, a large percentage of the units in the complex are for sale. Perusal of Hideaway newsletters and the community's annual magazine showed zero photos of children, suggesting that this is an older person's paradise, but paradise it is.

Madison Club

53035 Meriweather Way

La Quinta, Ca 92253
(760) 777-9320

The Madison Club presents itself especially well when you're driving up. There's no signage, just impressively tall scrubs, trees and a series of stone-surfaced buildings, one of them the guard shack, although it's in reality a small English gothic building like you might see at the University of Chicago or Yale. Sly Stallone once owned a place here because, scuttlebutt says, he was denied at the Vintage Club. Madison has a stunning clubhouse with sweeping stairs that leads to a second floor dining room and second floor dining room and

adjacent sushi bar and movie theater overlooking the golf course and mountains. Locker   rooms have full bars and lounges.The pro shop sells suits.

The spa gives mud and a dozen other types of massages. Little details matter here. For instance, golf balls at the club practice range come in supple leather bags. One-bedroom, 1,000

square foot clubhouse suites can be yours for $1M+. Lots are for sale   for $1 million to over $3 million. There will be 225 homes at build-out, but judging from what I saw, that's a long way off,   with over 190 build sites still available. There's currently a Madison estate on the market with an asking price of $30M.   The Tom Fazio golf course is in, the initiation fee $200K. Golf dues add $33,000 annually. Buy a place here and you'll have a long wait until there are enough people to populate many community activities, but what an entrance, and what luxurious privacy! In the meanwhile, because there aren't enough people   for a full activities calendar, owners here can join the social life available at the Hideaway, a sister property also developed by owner/developer Michael Meldman.

The Quarry

One Quarry Lane, La Quinta, CA 92253

(760) 777-1100

First some vital particulars: The Quarry was founded in 1994 and aptly named: It was once a rock quarry. The resulting topography makes for a spectacular chunk of real estate and an exotically beautiful Tom Fazio-designed 18-hole golf course that rises and falls as much as 300 feet filled with streams, sand traps, a waterfall, dips and curves. Golf Digest has rated it one of the world's 100 best. In 2002, a ten-hole, practice-facility/short course was added. Residents take advantage of sumptuous spa

treatment and steam rooms, a fitness center and indoor lap pool, which most high-end competitors don't offer. Cottages next to the clubhouse can be used for guests. Home asking prices run $1M to $7M. The exceptionally low monthly HOA is $440 and covers non-resident landscaping and security. A golf membership runs

$40K (less if you under age 50). Golf dues are $21,600 annually, up $2.4K   from last year, and annual Social dues run $10K per couple. There are still a few lots left for sale with asking prices $325K to $1.3M.

Toscana

43-199 Via Lucca

Indian Wells, CA (760) 404-1444

This tony Indian Wells community sits on relatively flat, uninteresting property but close to supermarkets and other retail shopping. The club's architecture is a magnificently executed mix of Tuscan and 'early California,' meaning lots of stone and exposed dark wood beams. You'll find attention to detail everywhere, to include flawless cobblestone walks and lush landscaping covering everything not a walkway, road or house. The tennis facilities include a clay court. There are no pickle ball courts, no indoor pool planned and no outdoor pool, suggesting this is not the club for you if you have children under the age of

25. Sales literature says the average resident age is 55. This seems a tad young. There's reportedly an out-sized contingent from Orange County, California. Because the builder (ubiquitous Bill Bone) is still subsidizing costs, Toscana is less expensive on a monthly basis than its competition and should remain so until build-out nine to ten years hence. Toscana's original 'seed' reportedly is super-rich LA businessman Peter Euberroth. House prices range from $900K to $2M +. If you want to build, lots cost around $500K, a golf membership $150K plus $1,750 monthly golf dues, and the equity sports club and spa $40K with $575 monthly dues. Toscana has just completed a second 18-hole

course. Apparently a second golf course outranks a swimming pool at Toscana.

The Reserve

14001 Reserve Drive
Indian Wells, CA 92210
(760) 568-559
thereserveclub.com

This 250-home gated community situated on 200 acres was opened in 1999. One source told me it was to handle 'overage' from the Vintage, which had filled up. Like the Vintage, the Reserves's

location in Indian Wells is close to high-end El Paseo restaurants and shops but located away from everybody in a quiet location flanked by The Living Desert and the Boyd Deep Canyon Research Center. Homes here run $1M to $6M. Bungalows, a group of three-bedroom homes close to the Clubhouse range from

2,559 to over 3,000 square feet; Casita Homes—3-and 4-bedroom zero-lot homes range from 3,150 to 3,750 square feet; Villas with 4000 to 5000+ square feet; and Estates, which sit on 3,000 to over 10,000SF lots. HOA's average $874 monthly. A golf membership costs $250K with golf dues an added $22.5K annually. Lots remain available with asking prices from $600K to $2M. I would imagine a $2M lot would have a great view of the valley and maybe even the Living Desert. I'd also imagine the price is negotiable. Unlike its competition, which tries to cover all its land with grass, trees

and shrubs, the Reserve prides itself on its embrace of indigenous terrain. It features among its amenities almost eight miles of

on-property walking trails. Over 1,700 trees were saved during course construction. The golf course includes foothills, small canyons and frequent views of the valley. A Tuscan-style bridge, a lake and lots of carefully chosen desert foliage. The restaurant has its own chef and a 500-bottle wine list.

The Thermal Club

86030 62nd Avenue

Thermal, CA 92274

760-239-6868

Do you have lots of money and love fast, exotic cars but don't

play golf? Tim Rodgers, owner of Tower Energy has hired Michael
Meldman, developer of La Quinta's high-end Madison and
Hideaway golf communities to market what may well be the
world's first true country club for car lovers --The Thermal Club,
it's located five miles west of La Quinta next to Jackie Cochran-
Desert Cities Airport. Thermal Club owners will enjoy a fleet of
race-prepped vehicles to drive. A phone call or email to the
concierge and it's arranged. You can store and have your cars
serviced at the site and schedule vehicle transport from anywhere.
BMW has established a Thermal Club performance center, one
of only two in the U.S., plus an M Club Driving School. High-

octane fuels are available plus restoration and tuning shops, parts center plus vintage and modern car servicing. The Control tower 'main clubhouse' will be ready in March 2016. Already operating are: (1) The Tuning Shop, driver's lounge and restaurant, locker rooms, restoration bays and a pro shop; (2) Trackside Garage with 40- car storage, a driving coaching/education room, drive-through car wash and detailing bay. A country-club-styled 'campus' with '

clubhouse, food & beverage, spa, fitness center, pool, hard courts and a Kids' Club. nears completion. 303 private memberships are available along with 270 lots off track and facing it. Some villa designs include villas with elevators and large garage bays for to 12 cars viewed from the living room through a glass roof. You'll be able to race motorcycles, go-karts and cars on 4.5 miles of racetrack in 20 different configurations. Memberships cost $85K up front with $9.2K yearly dues. You must pay $495K to $800K for a lot and build on it for a total of $1.3 to $3.4K. BMW's long-term commitment guarantees the project a healthy financial foundation. Gentlemen, start our engines!

Thunderbird Country Club

70-737 Country Club Drive
Rancho Mirage, CA 92270
(760) 328-2161

Unlike other high-end developments, the Thunderbird Country Club has no affiliation with surrounding Thunderbird-named gated communities, whose homeowners can join or not join the club. So technically, there is the stand-alone club and its abutting or nearby gated subdivisions, to include Thunderbird, Thunderbird Cove,

Thunderbird Villas, Thunderbird Palms, and Thunderbird Heights. Gerald and Betty Ford were Thunderbird members. Food is big here and can be found in the Grille Room, dining room, dining terrace, dining courtyard, Halfway House Grille and Men's and Ladies' Grille. There's a chef and more than decent wine cellar plus the usual golf, tennis, social mixers, and excellent fitness facilities in its own 6,000-square foot building with sauna, spa and massage therapy. The club was reportedly in decline by the 1990's but revitalized with a series of nice renovations.

Thunderbird is home to the Annenberg Estate, which is hidden from the outside world and Thunderbird Club members by a pink wall. Intimately associated with Thunderbird Country Club is Thunderbird Heights. It opened in rustily 1957. Asking prices

range from $750K to $7 million. It's called 'Heights' because it overlooks the Valley. President Obama was rumored to have bought a house here. So far, the rumors are unfounded. It is also rumored that he was outbid on a house but that his wife and children visited to check out another house. HOAs in Thunderbird Heights average $450 per month. Many of these homes have in recent years been total rebuilds. This gated community connects with the Thunderbird Country Club by underground tunnel under Highway 111.

The Tradition

78505 Old Avenue 52
La Quinta, CA 92253
(760) 563-8723

This gated community contains some oddities. There are no tennis courts, the only club I know of in the Coachella Valley that can say this, presuming it wishes to. Also, like the Vintage Club, there are no tee times. Show up for golf and you play. Opened in 1997, this 280-home development has homes with asking prices from $1.1M to $5M with lots going for $300K to $1.5M. Recent HOA's average $400 monthly. Golf memberships cost $200K with monthly dues of $1,950. A social membership costs $27.5K.

Tradition recently passed a big milestone –the developer finally turned over all assets to the members. Bungalow homes close to the clubhouse are available for guests. Tradition's homes

are 'lock and leave,' meaning their HOA of $1,075 monthly covers all costs associated with maintaining landscapes, pools, spas, fountains and pest control. Tradition has adopted a market-based pricing program allowing outgoing members to price their memberships. The Club will then offer an applicant the lowest price available on that month's resale list. So there is a possibility to get a great deal.

Vintage Club

75-001 Vintage Drive West I
Indian Wells, Ca. 92210
(760) 340-0500

The ultimate in prestige and name recognition, this club, founded
in the 1980s, is situated on 712 Indian Wells acres and home to
509 residences. Annual HOA dues run $3K. You'll pay $250K
for an equity golf membership, the only kind available, plus $32K
annually to play. The average house price exceeds $2M and the
average condo is estimated at $750,000+, although recently I
saw one advertised furnished for $650K. Some for-sale units
reportedly need major updating. The Vintage grounds are
meticulously maintained, there's a chef and great food.

During the November to May season, The Vintage is filled with famous and rich people who prize good manners and anonymity and find it inside the club's gates. The tone is WASP-ish, civil, collegial and restrained. No loud-mouth cigar smokers accepted. Members include Bill Gates (who owns a home supposedly purchased for his sister), Bill Gates' father, lee Iacocca, a Kelly of Kelly Blue Book fame, one of the Koch brothers and former Pimco CEO Bill Gross. No signage identifies the club's existence. Vintage members find that comforting.

Summary

Now that you've had a glimpse of the most expensive and assumed 'best' the Coachella Valley offers, you need to reflect on what 'best' may mean.

For starters, it means a large house on a large lot without houses crowding you. It means clubhouses built to look like Tuscan, Spanish and Mediterranean monasteries and palaces.

Grounds and facilities will be maintained immaculately. My son once visited the Vintage Club and saw workers cleaning the lily pads outside a clubhouse pond. That's the kind of micro care you can expect for your money.

A few of these communities have a Board that decides whether to accept you. This means you can agree to pay $9 million for a house, be approved by a bank but still be rejected.

The golf courses you play on may or may not be exceptional, but your treatment on them will be. Noise will be kept to a minimum. Some of these gated communities don't even have tee times. You play when you want.

Several 55+ communities have indoor pools and running tracks you won't find at all but one of these high-end communities.

On the other hand, these same 55+ communities won't have spas offering massages, mud baths and other pleasant treatments.

At a high-end community, a concierge will stock your pantry with groceries before you arrive. Your next-door neighbor might be famous.

As is true everywhere, there's a pecking order. The Vintage Club has perched at the top of the heap for   several decades but now has challengers. Some would argue it's been overtaken.

A friend of mine's girl friend, a personal trainer, told him that of all the high-end communities she'd worked, the Madison Club completely 'blew her mind.'

"Everything's so over-the-top luxurious, but in a good way," she said. "Everyone seems to be having so much fun." She concluded by saying it was clearly a place billionaires go to play.

On the negative side, The Madison Club struggles to gain members and create an indigenous social life. They have to go to the developer's companion club —The Hideaway—for that.

Toscana argues that it attracts a 'younger crowd' than its competition. This implies it's a good place to bring children; but it has no swimming pool, and most of its houses have three-bedrooms, which wouldn't work for three-child-and-up families. Hideaway's website and promotions also show no children.

All of this is mere quibbling. Each of these communities has a personality and amenities designed to pamper. The exorbitant costs of entry and maintaining a residence in any of them clearly aren't a barrier. Toscana alone sold 55 new homes in 2013 and almost 70 in 2015.

Drive through any of these developments and you'll see new houses being built, the area swarmed by workers making sure everything stays pristine. If you have the discretionary income, a desert high-end gated community will make you feel you've gone to heaven.

Comparison Chart
High-end Communities

Club	City	Price	Debut	Monthly HOA	Golf Initiation	Monthly golf dues	Number of home sites
Andalusia	La Quinta	$1.2 Million	2006	$650	$37.5K	$1,100	900
Big Horn	Palm Desert	$1.7 Million	1991	$700	$400K	$2K	570
El dorado	Indian Wells	$1M	1958	$2,000	$150K	$2,000	400
Griffin Ranch	La Quinta	$1M+	2014	$650	0	0	221
Hideaway	La Quinta	$1.7M	1993	$765	$150K	$2,125	292
Madison Club	La Quinta	$2M+	1992	$1,200	$200K	$2,917	225
The Quarry	La Quinta	$2M+	1994	$420	$50K	$2,167	100
Toscana	Indian Wells	$1M	2004	$490	$150K	$1,850	620
The Reserve	Indian Wells	$2M	1982	$874	$250K	$1,830	250
Thermal Club	Thermal	$1.3M	2014	***	0	0	201
Thunder-bird	Rancho Mirage	$2M+	1952	n/a	$50K	$1,871	Stand-alone club
Tradition	La Quinta	$800K	1997	$800	$125K	$2.250	290
Vintage	Indian Wells	$2M+	1985	$500+	$350K	$3,000	509

High-end Communities
Estimated total monthly expense

Community	HOA/golf	Monthly Utilities	est. Prop.Tax*	est Total
Madison	$4,117	$300	$1,000	$5,417
El Dorado	$3,835	$300	$1,000	$5,135
Vintage	$3,500	$300	$1,000	$4,800
The Reserve	$3,500	$300	$1,000	$4,800
Big Horn	$3,442	$300	$1,000	$4,747
Tradition	$3,050	$300	$1,000	$4,350

Average $4,315

Community	HOA/golf	Monthly Utilities	est. Prop.Tax*	est Total
Hideaway	$2,944	$300	$1,000	$4.214
Quarry	$2,587	$300	$1,000	$3,887
Toscana	$2,340	$300	$1,000	$3,640
Thunderbird	$2,235	$300	$1,000	$3,535
Andalusia	$1,750	$300	$1,000	$3,050
Thermal Club	$800	$300	$1,000	$2,100
Griffin Ranch	$650	$300	$1,000	$1,950

Note: The low monthly expense for both Griffen Ranch and The Terman Club is the result of no golf course or golf initiation fee and golf monthly dues.

NOTES

Do your own costing based on this model, plugging in your own numbers to see where you fit on the continuum shown above.

Keep in mind: Many high-end gated communities offer social memberships considerably less expensive than those golfers pay. The above estimates are for golf memberships only.

Remember: $ amounts show fixed on-going monthly expenses even   if you're not there.

Utilities (Gas/Electricity/Internet/Cable TV/Water) will average $300-$400 per month on average. Telephone, Internet and cable TV service may be purchased seasonally (November through May), but check to make sure as this may vary with provider and from city to city.

Maid service for a 2,000-square-foot house runs $75   every two weeks, or $150 per month. Double that for a 4,000-square-foot house.

A gardener will charge $85-$100 per month for a 2,000-square-foot house and double for a 4,000-square foot house, depending on the amount of landscaping.

If you have a pool, its maintenance will set you back a minimum of $100 per month.

CONCLUSION: :Owning a high-end house in a Coachella
Valley gated community, will hypothetically cost:

HOA/golf/utilities/property tax.......$4,600 monthly
Housekeeper............................. $300   "
Gardener................................. $200   "
Pool..................................... $100   "

              Grand total: **$5,200**   "

To comfortably operate your high-end home in the desert,
Budget $6K monthly.

The Upper Middle

Introduction
Upper middle houses are typically priced from $500,000 to $1,750,000

The primary differentiator between High End and Upper Middle gated communities is the cost of the golf initiation fee along with the average housing price, which may or may not reflect square footage and lot size.

Clubhouse, golf and exercise facilities are generally comparable. Houses may be closer together than in high-end communities and amenities such as a concierge may not be available, but a lot of personal service remains. You can also expect lower-priced but still relatively expensive condo clusters mixed in with large individual estates.

NOTE: *Statistics are taken from the public domain,   often realtor and gated community websites and a club's or HOA's general manager. I may be quoted a $ amount by an HOA official to learn that, say, in April, months after publication, rates have increased. I've made every effort to include the latest and most accurate data. Dues, fees and other costs are for 2016. If you spot an error, let me know at jbarnes3609@gmail.com.*

Desert Horizons

44900 Desert Horizons Drive
Indian Wells, CA 92210
(760) 340-1871

Ten years ago, this 510-home enclave might have been considered
High end. It's close to Palm Desert's El Paseo shopping and smack
in the middle of the desert's premier resort city, Indian Wells; but
recently too many homes seem to be for sale. Condo and home
prices range from $320K to $1.2M with HOA's of $695 monthly
and a non-transferable golf membership of $40K plus $1,330
monthly dues. The golf course opened in 1979 and the clubhouse
in 1980 and is 100% member-owned. Desert Horizons brands itself
as a club that offers more special events, dances and other goings-
on most if not all others. Is this true? I don't know. It does have its
own 18-hole

putting course, a three-mile perimeter biking route, five lighted tennis courts plus pickle ball and exercise   facilities. Its grill room stays open year around for breakfast and lunch. The main dining room closes during the summer. You can occasionally find a 2,500 square foot home here for the low to mid $400,000s.

Indian Ridge

76375 Country Club Drive

Palm Desert, CA 9221 (760) 772-7272

This relatively new gated golf community (est 1993) has 1,000 homes surrounded by beautifully manicured lawn and lovely

architecture, personalized service and housing that ranges from $400K condos to free-standing homes costing twice as much. HOAs run from $375 to $711 monthly. A Social membership costs $4K with $405 monthly dues. Equity golf memberships vary from $42.5K to $70K depending how much equity you want back when you leave. Golf dues will cost you $1,350 monthly. There's a concierge on premise, and 21 different free-standing home plans from 1,527 to 4,589SF. Grounds and maintenance equal anyone's.

Thirty-four pools are scattered throughout the community plus two 18-hole golf courses, four pickle ball courts and a basketball court. Tennis facilities (14 clay, grass and hard courts) are of highest quality. There's a spa. A member once told me about men in the bar bragging about their money, something that would be superfluous in a high end gated community. The experience

depressed her, she said, because she liked to think she'd bought in a place 'above' such pettiness. Apparently not. During season, the club holds lots of social mixers, BBQs and community dinners and can be a fun place. Out of season, not so much.

Indian Wells Country Club

46000 East Eldorado Drive
Indian Wells, CA 92210
(760) 345-2561

One of the oldest and formerly most prestigious country clubs in the Coachella Valley, Indian Wells Country Club is one of the better values, its cost of membership comparable to mid-priced clubs with the added prestige of its name and location. It offers members a beautiful clubhouse along with first-class amenities. The Club underwent a major re-do in 2001. Recent home and condo values range from $220K to $2 million. HOA dues vary by development, but figure $550 as an average. In all, 900 condos and freestanding homes have been built, with construction beginning

in the 1950's and ending in 2013. The condos are nice enough but even the updated ones seem from another era. They range from

1,776 to 3,000 square feet. Pools are scattered about the various condo communities. Prices are impressively low for such a fine facility. A non-transferable golf membership costs only $17K with $950

monthly dues. If you're under 50, your initiation drops to $7.5K with $554 monthly dues. A Social/Fitness membership will set you back $500 with $231 monthly dues. This Club's location off Avenue 111 is close to shopping. If location's important to you, a decent condo here might be had for $350K along with the Indian Wells address. Plus you'll enjoy a country club that will impress your most cynical friends.

Ironwood Country Club

73735 Irontree Drive

Palm Desert, CA (760) 346-0551

This 800-acre development has been busy throughout 2015. It's

now in the process of converting 40 of its acres to deserts cape, has added two pickle ball courts, a bocce ball court and re-finished and improved its fitness center. Ironwood is a large community with 1,050 residences. Home values run from the high $200Ks to $3M with monthly HOA dues of $480 to $710. Opened in 1974, it includes 16 different homeowner groups, each with its own management, reserve fund, etc. In addition to the new pickle ball courts, residents have access to three tennis courts plus a stadium court, a Tuscan-style clubhouse and fitness center plus spa.

Ironwood's two golf courses are open to the public and include an 18-acre parcel with driving range and practice holes for working on one's short and long game. The south course has no homes facing directly on it. The equity golf initiation fees that 15 years

ago would have cost you $50K and up now costs $17K with monthly $1,520 dues. A tennis/fitness/social membership costs $2K plus $406 monthly, a sore point with members. I've run into three tennis players recently who bought cheaper social memberships at the nearby Shadow Mountain Resort and even nearer Palm Desert Tennis Club. In season, Ironwood residents can join hiking, ballroom dancing, tap dancing, cycling, putting, Mah-jongg, cooking, wine tasting, bridge and gin rummy groups plus a guest speaker series, so there's plenty to do.

La Quinta Resort and Club

49-499 Eisenhower Drive
La Quinta, CA 92253
(760) 564-4111

www.laquintaresort.com

The La Quinta Resort and Club started in1926 as a cluster of rental bungalows and is now considered the oldest resort in the valley. My son, his wife and three young children like to vacation weekends here. They can rent and together stay in a cottage there, use a nearby swimming pool, relax and enjoy Morgan's, an excellently reviewed restaurant on premise, play tennis, golf, listen to music and go dancing at night. However, when asked if he'd

like to buy a condo or house there, he said, "No. Too much traffic and too many people moving in and out each day." That's the La Quinta Resort and Club's problem. Now owned by The Waldorf Corporation, several previous owners have gone bankrupt trying to sell homes while running a resort. There are tennis villas and small condos available. Offering prices have risen, some 1600-square-foot condos now for sale for upwards of $1M, but predictably, sales haven't risen. The resort by itself offers guests 796 casitas, 41 swimming pools, 23 tennis courts, seven restaurants and 90 holes of golf on-site and five adjoining PGA communities that also utilize La Quinta Resort and Club facilities: The Citrus Club, Enclave, Enclave Mountain, Haciendas at La Quinta Resort, and the La Quinta Country Club. On the next pages you'll find descriptions of each of these separate but linked developments.

Bajada Estates

Dry Creek Road south of Avenue 50

La Quinta, CA 92253

This non-golf subdivision has homes priced at $500K to $600K running 2,000 to 3,000 square feet. The development was opened in 1995 and has a low monthly HOA of $175. Golf and Social memberships are   available through the Citrus Club (See next page), which includes use of its clubhouse plus nine PGA West and La Quinta Club and Resort courses.

The Citrus Club

50-503 Mandarina

La Quinta, Ca 92253

(760) 564-7620

Adjacent to the public La Quinta Resort and Club and designated this Resort's attached private club, Citrus began building houses in 1987. The development's 576 home owners get access to the La Quinta Resort's golf courses, courses,tennis, fitness and other facilities. Asking prices average $450K to $1M+. The HOA runs

$250 to $500 monthly. A non-transferable golf membership costs 30K with monthly dues $1,134, which includes full privileges at nine La Quinta Resort and PGA PGA West golf courses. A Social membership costs $5K with $327 monthly dues, and allows use of the Resort's, Citrus' and PGA West's dining, fitness facilities and tennis. The Citrus Club has yet to sell all its lots. In fact, this Spring, a developer opened what he calls 'The Cove at Citrus,' with homes selling in the $700K to $900K range.

Enclave Estates

49-499 Eisenhower Drive
La Quinta, CA 92253
(760) 564-4111

www.laquintaresort.com

This La Quinta Golf and Resort development was built between 1990 and 2006. Build-able lots still remain. Homes range from 3,000 to 7,000 square feet priced from the $900Ks to $3M. HOA dues range from $375 to $800 monthly. Modern, Spanish and Tuscan styles predominate. These homes get La Quinta Resort and Club's room and laundry services plus charging privileges there. Enclave and Enclave Mountain are separately gated. Residents also can use Citrus Club clubhouse and its Golf and Social packages.

Enclave Mountain Estates

49-499 Eisenhower Drive
La Quinta, CA 92253
(760) 564-4111
www.laquintaresort.com

This 32-home community sits separately gated within Enclave's gates (*See previous page*). Sun Microsystems' Scott McNealy is said to have a home here, although such celebrity info tends to be highly unreliable and often behind the times. Golf memberships run $100K with $700 monthly dues. HOAs are $375 monthly. The average home costs $3M+. All are over 4,000 square feet and have four or five bedrooms. The La Quinta Resort and Club Membership desk handles sales. Citrus Club clubhouse and Golf/ Social packages are available.

La Quinta Fairways

Avenue 50 and Park

La Quinta, CA 92253

Built from 1991 to 2001, this gated community's 250 one- and two-story homes are sized from 2,000 to 3,000 square feet and are priced from $375K to $750K. HOA dues run $284 monthly. Most units face either the Pete Dye Course managed by the La Quinta Resort and Club or a large lake.

Haciendas at La Quinta Resort

Avenue 50 east of Eisenhower Drive

La Quinta, CA 92256

This small 65-home development features 3- and 4-bedroom homes running 2,320 to 2,283 square feet with pool/spa costing $450K to $1M+. The HOA runs $165 plus $245 monthly for access to the La Quinta Resort and Club's tennis and fitness facilities, along with 'preferred' rates at the Resort's five affiliated golf courses.

Legacy Villas

49-499 Eisenhower Drive
La Quinta, CA 92253 (760) 564-4111
www.laquintaresort.com

These These 280, two-story condo homes on the La Quinta Club Resort campus are designed with separate entrances to accommodate rentals and range from 1,307 to 1,706 square feet. They were built in 2005. Prices run from $200K to $500K. The HOA is $729 per month. Citrus Club clubhouse and its Golf and Social packages are available.

Los Estados

49-499 Eisenhower Drive
La Quinta, CA 92253
(760) 564-4111
www.laquintaresort.com

The address for Los Estates is actually that of the La Quinta Resort and Club. Why? Because this subdivision faces the Resort's mountain course and use of the Resort's Golf and Social memberships originate there or through the Citrus Club (Page 120). There are 40 single-family, 3- and 4-bedroom, 2,400 to 3,500 square-foot homes in this subdivision. The HOA runs $455 monthly.

Painted Cove

Avenue 50 and Park Avenue

La Quinta, CA 92253

This subdivision, opened in 1991, has 76 three- and four-bedroom homes sized from 2,792 to 4,000 square feet. Recent sales have tended to fall in the $550K to 975K range. The HOA runs $221 monthly. A non-golf community, Golf and Social memberships are available through The Citrus Club (Page 120).

Palmilla Estates

Avenue 50 near Jefferson Street

La Quinta, CA 92253

This non-golf community adjacent to the Citrus Club features contemporary homes mixed in with seven acres of lakes and streams. The homes were built between 2002 and 2005 and are on the large side —2,894 to 4,613 square feet— and sell for between $750K and $1.3M. The HOA is currently $620 monthly. Residents are eligible to buy a Golf or Social membership at the Citrus Club across the street.

Point Happy Estates

Washington Avenue south of Highway 111

La Quinta, CA 92253

This gated, non-golf subdivision of 69 three- and four-bedroom homes sized from 2,800 to 3,800 square feet was built in 2005. Resales have been running $700K to $900K. The HOA is a low $250 per month. Golf and Social memberships are available through the Citrus Club (Page 120).

Santa Rosa Cove

Jefferson at Avenue 50

La Quinta, CA 92253

This La Quinta Resort and Club companion development broke
ground in 1982 and was sold out by 1992. Homes run 1,389 to
2,475 square feet and cost $300K to $600K. HOA dues cost $475
monthly. Golf and Social memberships are purchased
through the Citrus Club or PGA West membership desks.

Spa Villas

49-499 Eisenhower Drive
La Quinta, CA 92253
(760) 564-4111

www.laquintaresort.com

It's hard to figure the price points on these residences. They sit on a private street and area on the La Quinta Resort and Club campus and are sized from 934 to 2,400 square feet and on the market for

$650K to $1.4M! Each house is sold turn-key furnished and, if the owner wishes, can be added to the resort's Waldorf Astoria Properties' rental lists. All have been on the market awhile. Most are rented out when possible.

La Quinta Resort Tennis Villas

49-499 Eisenhower Drive

La Quinta, CA 9225

This 48-unit development adjacent to the La Quinta Resort and Club tennis shop, lounge and pro shop has units sized from 1,627 to 1,931 square feet that sell for $400K to $675K with an HOA of $570 monthly. Many of these units are rented out in season. Social and Golf memberships at the Resort or Citrus Club must be purchased separately and made available to guests and renters.

La Quinta Country Club

77-750 Avenue

La Quinta, Ca 92256

(760) 564=4151

Once part of the La Quinta Resort and club, members purchased one of the golf courses in 1977 and founded La Quinta Country Club. A clubhouse followed only to be almost completely redone in 'Santa Barbara' style in 2009. Like the Thunderbird Golf Club (See High-end section, Page 91), the La Quinta Country Club is not an integrated part of a gated community. The condos, built in the '60's and 70's range upwards from 1,700 square feet cost in the mid $200K's and tend to have only one full bath. They go

by names such as Golf Estates and Lago La Quinta. Montego Estates consists of custom homes of 3,000 square feet and more. Home prices range from $250,000 to $3 million. Because these homes tend to be old with prices much lower than comparable newer properties in PGA West and surrounding communities. A La Quinta Country Club equity golf membership costs $45K with half that amount returned when sold. Monthly golf dues run $1,650 per month. Junior memberships can be had for $12.5K with $825 monthly dues. Social

memberships cost $5K with $542 monthly dues. There are trout-stocked lakes on premise plus the usual fitness center, tennis courts, spa services, etc. for members to use and enjoy.

Surrounding La Quinta Country Club golf course communities

Even long-time residents of the Coachella Valley have a hard time figuring out which communities are attached to the La Quinta Resort and Club and which are privy to the La Quinta Country Club.

To help you figure this out, imagine the following time line: A developer builds the La Quinta Resort and Club on open land in what is now La Quinta. Decades later, the La Quinta Country Club breaks off from the La Quinta Resort and Club, builds its own club house to support its own golf club and becomes a separate entity.

So now you have two stand-alone communities —The La Quinta Resort and Club, and the La Quinta Country Club.

To separate owners from renters, the La Quinta Resort and Club sets up a private gated community with its own clubhouse —the Citrus Club.

Land that surrounds or intersects the La Quinta Country Club, La Quinta Resort, the Citrus and their golf courses is sold to different developers who build separate gated communities. s a result, you get independent gated developments whose residents can, for a price, use the La Quinta Resort and Club's clubhouse or the facilities or those of the The Citrus Club and/or the La Quinta Resort and Club.. If a particular gated community listed on the following pages interest you, check to see whose golf courses, club houses and other amenities are available. Some communities will even offer you a choice between La Quinta Resort and Club amenities, those of the Citrus Club, the La Quinta Country Club or PGA West, Pages 129, 132 and 145.

Duna La Quinta

Avenue 50 at Avenida Los Verde
La Quinta, CA 92253

Facing the La Quinta Resort and club, these condos built in the mid 1980's run 1,700 to 3,200 square feet. Prices fall between $250K and $600K, with the typical unit having approximately 2,000 square feet and selling in the low $300K's. The per-square-foot prices here are lower than elsewhere in the Valley because the homes are older, many have changed hands many times or are rentals and need updating. HOAs are $460 per month.

Hidden Canyon

77928 Desert Drive
La Quinta, CA 92253

On Eisenhower Drive, this gated community of 169 three-, four- and five-bedroom homes opened and sold out between 2005 and

2006. Single-family homes cost $650- to $900K and are sized from 2,390- to 3,600 square feet. HOA monthly dues are $200, which is exceptionally low for the Desert. Homes back up to the Santa Rosa Mountains. Social and Golf memberships are available at the La Quinta Resort and Club across the street.

Lago La Quinta

77-750 Avenue
La Quinta, Ca 92256
(760) 564=4151

Located within the La Quinta Country Club, this development broke ground in 1959 and consists of two- and three-bedroom condos ranging from 2,300- to 3,000 square feet costing $300- to $400K. Monthly HOA dues run $490. Most condos face a lake. In addition, the community offers three community pools and a tennis court. You get more square footage for the dollar here than most places in the desert because the units are so old.

Laguna La Paz

Eisenhower near Avenue 50
La Quinta, CA 92253

Built and sold from 1984 to 1995, this 400-home development, a mix of condos, free-standing and attached residents offers two- and three-bedroom homes priced from $300K to $500K and ranging from 1,600 to 2,300 square feet. Monthly HOA dues run $550. On the premises you'll find 15 community pools, 15 spas, five tennis courts with lights, a clubhouse, two paddle boats and an electric boat to move about the seven-acre lake, a putting green and abundant walkways. This gated community is located adjacent to both the La Quinta Resort and Club and the La Quinta Country Club.

Montero Estates

Washington Street at Avenue 50
La Quinta, CA 92253

Built in the 1970's and 2980's, this 59-home community located at the southeastern perimeter of the La Quinta Country Club grounds has seen falling prices in recent years. The good news: Many of these two- and three-bedroom 1,620 to 2,900 square feet homes cost $250- to $650K and face the La Quinta Country Club golf course. The HOA runs $300 to $475 monthly depending on the home Its located adjacent to the La Quinta Country Club.

La Quinta Country Club Villas

77-750 Avenue

La Quinta, Ca 92256

(760) 564=4151

By now you've gathered that most of the housing stock associated with the La Quinta Country Club dates from the 1960's and '70's. So it goes with this 40-unit condo development, which sits facing the golf course and offers pleasant views. Homes range from 1,368 to 1,558 square feet and sell for between $275 and $400K depending on the amount of updating done. The monthly HOA runs $395 but sales are few and rentals are many. There's a community pool but for amenities you have to join the La Quinta Country club that's a short walk or bike ride away.

Mission Hills Country Club

34-600 Mission Hills Drive
Rancho Mirage, CA 92270
(760) 324-940
missionhillssales.com/index.html

This 1,760-acre development began in 1966 with the country club. Over time, different developers added 1,500 condo- and freestanding-homes, each with its own homeowner association. Most of these residences get

reduced fees to join Mission Hills either as a Social or Golf member. The club offers three golf courses, one of tournament caliber. A Social membership includes what are arguably the finest private tennis facilities in the Coachella Valley.

A 90% refundable golf membership costs $65K and a non-refundable one $45K. Monthly dues run $1,088 for either. A Sports Club membership (tennis, pickle ball, croquet and fitness center) runs $2.5K with $329 monthly dues. A Social membership (which includes clubhouse social activities and discounts at its restaurants) costs $1K with monthly $234 dues.

The Mission Hills' various associated gated developments offer $2.9-million estates at the high end and low-end condos selling for $180,000 to $375K. This huge price spread makes this community tough to place in a hierarchy. Its condo housing prices place it in 'the middle.' Its $ million-plus-home enclaves place it in the 'high-end.' A compromise was needed, so I've placed Mission Hills in Upper middle, but that may be too high. Its older condos are

a 'tough sell.' One woman told me that every activity was annoyingly à la carte. She said she was waiting until she was old enough to buy into a 55+ community. "My problem," she said, "is that condo prices here keep dropping." That said, you don't hear similar complaints from people living in Mission Hills' $1M+ estates.

Mission Hills East

34-600 Mission Hills Drive
Rancho Mirage, CA 92270
(760) 324-9400
missionhillssales.com/index.html

This development of 370 condos and homes (1,300 to 2,736 square feet) was built between 1987 and 1991 and overlooks the Westin Hotel and Resort's Pete Dye golf course. Most prices sit between $300K and $500K. HOAs are $488. You own your own land. Mission Hills Country club amenities are available but aren't included   in the HOA, meaning you'll pay the going rate for any or all of them.

Mission Hills Tennis Villas

34-600 Mission Hills Drive
Rancho Mirage, CA 92270
(760) 324-9400
missionhillstennisvillas.com

Two-hundred-twenty-one tennis villas are located on Racquet Club Drive near the tennis complex. They were built from 1971 to 1989. Prices run from the mid $150K to the mid $300,000s and range from 1,050 to 1615 square feet. HOAs average $500+ per month. Be aware that in addition, there's a yearly $3,450 payment due because these villas sit on leased land.

Mission Hills Custom Home Developments
Fairway Estates

34-600 Mission Hills Drive
Rancho Mirage, CA 92270
(760) 324-9400

missionhillssales.com/index.html

Fairway Estates homes were built in 1989. Each is different and overlooks the private Arnold Palmer golf course. Some of these homes reach 10,000 square feet in size and go for $2 million and

up. Build-able lots remain available. HOA dues currently run $365 monthly.

Lakefront I and II Homes run from 1,986 to 2,142 square feet, are lake-facing and may or may not sit on leased land. HOA dues run $543 monthly and include a Mission Hills Tennis membership. Home prices run $500K to $800K.

Legacy Oakhurst's 156 homes rest on 126.5 private acres overlooking Mission Hills' Dinah Shore Golf Course and run from 2,500 to 3,500 square feet with asking prices from the low $700,000s to $1.3 million. The monthly HOA runs $592, which includes use of Mission Hills' clubhouse facilities and Fitness

center.

Mira Vista's 307 homes, built from approximately 2003 to 2005, face Mission Hills' Gary Player Golf Course and include their own community pool. Homes run $550K to almost $1M. HOA's run $303 monthly.

Stone Ridge's 45 fairway homes on the Mission Hills Pete Dye course, developed from 1999 to 2000, range from 2,549 to 3,169 square feet with asking prices from the low $700Ks to high $900Ks. HOA dues are $370 and include a Mission Hills Social membership.

Twenty-one **Mission Haciendas** face the Mission Hills Pete Dye course. They were constructed between 1989 and 2005 and run 3015 to 3079 square feet. Their prices average in the $800K's. HOAs run $303 monthly.

Westgate, a newer development, with houses and lots for sale since 2007, includes 32 homes facing Mission Hills' Pete Dye course. HOAs are $421 monthly. Home prices run from $500K to $800K.

Morningside Country Club

39033 Morningside Drive

Rancho Mirage, CA 92270

(760) 324-1234

This club recently spent $1.5M re-doing its fitness center and spa and adding a wrap-around deck to its main restaurant for al fresco dining overlooking the golf course. Morningside opened in 1981. Its 363 houses range from 2,900 to almost 6,000 square feet and have asking prices from $600,000 to $1.6 million+. A golf membership costs $50K with $1,862 monthly dues. An Associates membership for those under 55 has the same initiation fee but

lowers the monthly dues to $931. The HOA runs an additional

$1,050 monthly. This includes cable TV, annual roof cleaning and exterior painting of individual homes every five years or so. The club's website brags that its membership includes former U.S. presidents, industry titans, sports luminaries and others equally famous from the arts and professions. This makes me suspicious. The Vintage Club, Madison Club and Big Horn can certainly make such membership claims but don't. You wonder if Morningside may be trying to 'box above its weight class.' The community does offer some special amenities, to include an on-site handyman, a 24-hour concierge shuttle service and annual

The Morningside clubhouse.

renewal of over 10,000 new flats of flowers each Fall. Its unseemly bragging aside, Morningside is one of those gated communities that rate at the high end of the Upper Middle category.

Mountain View Country Club
80-375 Pomelo
La Quinta, CA 92253
(760) 771-4311

This 426-home Toll Brothers gated community opened in 2005 with a mix of condos and freestanding homes. The condos run $350,000 to $600,000 and the houses $600K to $1.5M. A golf membership costs a non-refundable $31K and comes included in the price of   some properties, so if you're interested, make sure to check. Golf dues run $1,025 monthly. Along with your golf membership come reciprocal privileges at 114   similar facilities across the nation. Homes have from 2,500 to 4,000 square feet. Condo sizes are predictably smaller (1,746 to 2,103SF). Condo HOA dues currentlyrun $618 monthly while freestanding home HOAs cost less ($400 monthly). One realtor website I saw indicated homeowners paid two HOAs, one for their condo or house area and the other for the common grounds. Check to see if this is accurate. If you don't opt for a golf membership, you're required to purchase a Social membership instead, but if you're buying a re-sale home, it's included in the purchase price. Social dues run $409 monthly. There's lovely Spanish architecture, a

spa, steam room, pub and restaurant. The club's web site lists a multitude of resident activities to include a book club, something called 'Desert Dogs Cycling,' hiking, investment, bible study, canasta, bridge and various golf activities. The club's executive chef previously held the same title at both the Ritz Carlton and Vintage Club.

The Palms

57000 Palms Drive
La Quinta, CA 92253
(760) 771-0297

This gated community differs from other Upper-middle clubs in that it doesn't attempt to be 'all things to all people,' which, as explained to me, means it considers itself a 'secondary' club that concentrates solely on golf. When asked what this meant, I was told that many Palms members belong to other clubs but fly in, find they can't get tee times when they want; so they go to the Palms. Is this true? Do some rich people really join two golf communities in the desert? I have no idea. Founded in 1999, the Palms' 104-home development (at build-out) is named for its 2,000+ palm trees, which are just part of this community's charm. The Palms also offers a multitude of mesquite and citrus trees and once was a farm. Eighty homes face on the golf course. Their sizes range from 2,493 to 6,500 square feet. Lots remain for sale. Home prices range from $500K to $1.7 million, with HOA dues $335 monthly. Lots go for $150,000 to $400,000. A golf membership costs $20K with monthly $745 dues, up $110 in the past two years. The exercise facilities could use an upgrade. There's a restaurant on premise but no pickle ball, tennis or bocce ball. It's strictly golf. One especially nice feature: no tee times. Show up and you play.

PGA West

55-955 PGA Boulevard
La Quinta, CA 92255
(760) 564-7111
www.pgawest.com

PGA West consists of seven separate gated condo and freestanding home clusters totaling 2,941 residences, each cluster attached to a golf course and sharing a large centrally located tennis and exercise complex, clubhouse and restaurants. HOA monthly dues vary but run between $500 and $800 monthly depending on the size of the residence. The entire development comprises 2,200 acres, making PGA West the largest golf and leisure complex in the California desert. These developments (The first opened in

d1984) are treated as a single entity because they share the same parent corporation and many abut one another. **A golf membership for any of the PGA West gated communities listed in this book costs $45K with $1,249 monthly dues.** That lets you play on three public and three private golf courses, 108 holes in all. Residents can use PGA West's tennis, golf, gym and pickle ball facilities. I chatted with a man who'd moved to a 55+ community after living in PGA West's Arnold Palmer development. He'd bought a Social membership for $24K and was supposed to get all of it back when he left. 'They' gave him half. He remains bitter. Otherwise, he says, PGA West was a nice place to live. If you like the PGA West concept, here's what's available:

The PGA West Greg Norman gated community opened in 1999 has no condos and is the smallest but priciest, its freestanding homes priced from $700,000 to $1,300.000.

PGA West Legends gated community has 625 $500K to $1.3M homes, also with no condos. The golf course and home building beganin 1999.

The PGA West Tom Weiskopf gated community opened in 1996 has single-family residences in the $500,000 to $2,000,000 range. No condos. Its HOA runs $305-$635 monthly

PGA West Jack Nicklaus Private Course gated community's condos run $400K to $700K and homes from $500K to $2.2M. The course was completed in 1987and home building around it commenced soon after.

The PGA West Pete Dye Stadium Course gated community holds 625 condos selling for from $220,000 to $700,000 with freestanding homes $550K to $2M. It opened in 1987.

The PGA West Jack Nicklaus Tournament Course gated community, completed in 1987, offers condos costing $200K to $500K and houses that run $500K to $1.5M.

PGA West's Arnold Palmer gated community, completed in 1998, features condos starting around $200K and top out at $900K, with houses priced from $400K to $1.2M.

To conclude: There's a sameness and blurring of identity to all the PGA West communities. Do residents living in $220K condos have much in common with residents paying over $1M? Doubtful. Constant changes in PGA West corporate ownership plus a bankruptcy create an additional worry.

he PGA West Residence Club

54-500 West Residence Club Drive
La Quinta, CA
(760)-771-2070 (888)-650-9200
www.residenceclubpgawest.com

You're looking at what's touted as a $1M PGA West home available as a 1/9th or 1/4th-of the year time-share, one of 32 such homes in this development. Each home comes fully furnished with three bedrooms, private attached casita, heated pool, 3.5 baths and 3,365 square feet. If you golf, you'll pay the $45K golf equity membership initiation but don't get to prorate the $1.2K+ monthly dues. Or, you can play public or semi-public courses and forego such costs. You'll get on-site concierge   services to stock your refrigerator before you arrive plus you'll pay a monthly $1,090 HOA fee for landscape upkeep, property taxes, insurance, utilities, security, house keeping and a 'reserve' contribution for replacing items as they age. Residence Club homes have been available since 2006, yet some time-shares are still available on new homes, suggesting that demand isn't brisk. In late September, 2015, I checked r esales and found a 1/9th share available for $90K, reduced from its original asking price of 125K. The resale had already been on the market 179 days.

Montera at The Greg Norman

56150 PGA Boulevard La Quinta, CA 92253

760-771-2100

Positioned within the Greg Norman residential development, this 2,000-acre new 39-home development features large home sites of from 9,200 to 15,000 square feet that include 300 to 650 square feet of covered outdoor living space.. The architecture is the predictable Tuscan and Spanish colonial. Homes range from 3,180 to 3,624 square feet. Starting prices begin at around $800K and top

out close to $1M. A pool and spa are included with every home. No news yet on likely HOA costs but you can assume they'll range somewhere in the middle to upper middle within PGA West's $300 to $800 average monthly HOA charge. If you're tempted to buy here, figure $40-$60K in add-ons to get the finishes and landscaping you prefer.

Signature at PGA West

56-150 PGA Boulevard
La Quinta, CA
(760) 564-3991
signaturewestatpgawest.com

This relatively small 44.95-acre development is reputedly the last slice of PGA West open land available for development. It's directly across from the PGA West clubhouse main entrance and at build-out will contain 230

condos and free-standing homes. Twenty-three spec homes are ready for sale ranging from $423K to $890K sized from 1,446 to 3,479 square feet. These homes will be placed in three distinct and separate neighborhoods –attached villas (read 'condos'), haciendas and estates. All will share a gate manned 24 hours. To spur buying, up to $35K in upgrades are being offered as of November 2015. Paying $400K+ for a 1,446-square-foot condo seems steep. I suspect these prices are negotiable.

Rancho La Quinta Country Club

79295 Rancho La Quinta Drive
La Quinta, CA
(760) 777-7792

Called "Rancho" by residents, this development's 900 homes and 85 condos on 700 acres broke ground in 1993 on one golf course and in 2000 on a second. The HOA runs $675 monthly. All homes surround the racquet club or golf course. Home values run $400K to $1.6M sized from 2,635 to 2,924 square feet. Social/Fitness memberships are included in the HOA dues. There are nine lighted tennis courts, two of them clay, and one a stadium court. You can dine court side in season. You'll pay $105K for a refundable equity golf membership or $39.5K for a nonrefundable one. Oddly, unlike most other clubs, no pickle ball courts are available. Golf dues are $1,325 monthly, up $100 from the previous year. There's also a one-year 'trial' golf membership available. for $15,500. Lots of picturesque lakes, streams, rocks and rills make Rancho La Quinta a pleasant place to walk. The community had approximately 60 resales in the past year, or a turn-over of six percent, suggesting a stable long-term and satisfied resident community.

The Rancho La Quinta clubhouse.

Tamarisk

70240 Frank Sinatra Drive
Rancho Mirage, CA 92270
(760) 328-2141

Throughout 2015, Tamarisk, one of the Valley's older clubs, has been aggressive in curbing water usage, installing sensors that

register when an area needs water so that grassy areas can be spot-treated. In addition, the club's acreage fronting on Frank Sinatra has been converted from grass to desertscape. Tamarisk was open to Jews at a time when other clubs discriminated against them and 60 years later still maintains a 'Jewish vibe' with kosher-style foods on the menu. A non-transferable golf membership costs $30K with $1,554 monthly dues. A social membership runs $15K with $777 monthly dues, and if you're 55 or younger, you can join for $10K.

Tamarisk is a standalone country club. House prices in unaffiliated adjacent subdivisions range from the mid $300,000s to $1.5 million-plus. The HOAs vary. There's reported to be a large contingent of Chicago Jewish 'aristocracy' who belong to Tamarisk and winter in nearby subdivisions, where homes average between 2,500 and 5,500 square feet. According to a 2014 series of articles in the local <u>Desert Sun,</u> Frank Sinatra and several high-ranking members of Jewish and Italian Mafias were once members in the 1970's and '80s. I'm told by a Tamarisk member that back then

Sinatra would occasionally show up at club functions and sing. The club is beginning to look 'tired' and there's rumors of 'age creep.' A thorough renovation of the clubhouse and grounds is supposedly 'in the works.' Does this mean members will be assessed extra to make this happen? Stay tuned.

Summary

Many Upper middle communities come close to equaling their High-end brethren in amenities and distinctiveness. Million-dollar-plus houses can be found in both. Clubhouse architecture is more often than not similarly impressive. So what separates the Upper middle from the High-end? Mostly the price of Golf and Social Initiation fees, which in Upper Middle communities can be a third of what High-end clubs charge. Also, High-end complexes tend to have fewer members.' High-end communities have Boards that can exclude those they don't like. This can happen in Upper middle gated developments but occurs less often if at all. High-end community residents further separate themselves by their indifference to costs. In addition to paying HOA dues as high as $32,000 annually, they sponsor and give to desert charities, build extra golf holes and tear down the interior a clubhouse because they're tired of it and want something new.

If status and the wealth of your fellow residents is of no concern, you can avoid both High-end and Upper middle clubs, save money and get equivalent facilities in mid-priced communities, although if you spend time in each type of development you'll notice 'differences.' In some ways, deciding where to buy a home in the Desert is like buying a car. You can spend $30K and get an automobile with a 185-horsepower engine equipped almost identically with a similarly sized car with a 400-horsepower costing three to five times as much. Your $150K car will have $5-6K more spent on its interior but will sport the same lane-changing and collision warnings, etc. as the $30K car while getting worse gas mileage. So why pay $150K for basically the same car? Because your purchase documents to others that you can.Using that same logic, why pay $250K for a golf membership and a 4,800 square foot house costing $1.2M when you can get the same size house for the same money and pay only $50K for a golf membership? Perhaps because we are often judged by the company we prefer.

COMPARISON CHART
Upper-Middle Gated Communities

Community	City	Price	Debut	HOA	Fee	Dues	Homes
Desert Horizons	IW	$650K	1979	$650	$25K	$1,200	510
Indian Ridge	PD	$750K	1993	$400	$70K	$1,335	1,068
Indian Wells CC	IW	$500K	1956	$550	$25K	$974	900
Ironwood	PD	$750K	1974	$300	$28K	$1,319	1,050
La Quinta Resort & Club	LQ	$500K	1926		$100K	$1,053	1,800 associated home subs
Citrus Club	LQ	$600K	1987	$495	$100K	$1,053	625
La Quinta Country Club	LQ	$500K	1959	$450	$25K	$1,513	1,100 associated home subs
Mission Hills communities	RM	$500K	1972	$500	$30K	$1,040	1,500 associated home subs
Morning side	RM	$750K	1989	$1,000	$50K	$1,408	363

Mountain View	LQ	$750K	2002	$580	$75K	$928	426
The Palms	;Q	$750K	1999	$335	$20K	$745	104
PGA West communities	LQ	$500K	1984	$500	$45K	$1,249	2,941 associated home subs
Rancho La Quinta	LQ	$750K	1993	$785	$30K	$1,225	600
Tamarisk	RM	$500	1951	$750	$30K	$1,450	Stand-alone club

*** The individual home $ amount and HOA listed for Indian Wells Country Club, La Quinta Resort and Club, La Quinta Country Club, Mission Hills and PGA West communities reflects a mid-point. Communities attached to these developments can have homes priced as low as $200K to as high as $3M and HOAs greater or less than shown..

Upper-middle Communities
Estimated total monthly expense

Community	HOA/Golf	Utilities	Est^. Prop. Tax	Est.^ Total Monthly
Morningside	$2,408	$300	$750	$3,485
Tamarisk	$2,200	$300	$750	$3,250
Rancho La Quinta	$2,010	$300	$750	$3,060
La Quinta Country Club	$1,963	$300	$750	$3,013
Desert Horizons	$1,850	$300	$750	$2,900
Indian Ridge	$1,735	$300	$750	$2,785
		Average: $2,763		
Ironwood	$1,619	$300	$750	$2,669
Citrus Club	$1,576	$300	$750	$2,625
Indian Wells CC	$1,524	$300	$750	$2,574
Mountain View	$1,508	$300	$750	$2,558
Mission Hills CC	$1,450	$300	$750	$2,500
PGA West	$1,425	$300	$750	$2,475
The Palms	$970	$300	$750	$2,020

Notes

PGA Legends, Tom Weiskopf, Greg Norman, Jack Nicolas Private, Pete Dye Stadium, Jack Nicolas Tournament,Arnold Palmer Monterra, Residence and Signature developments all have the same HOA/Golf monthly charges.

Tamarisk and Mission Hills are stand-alone clubs with no HOA.

300 utility average is speculative and differs by Coachella Valley city and individual home usage. Actual monthly expense could be more or less.

Be aware

These $ amounts show fixed on-going monthly expenses <u>even if you're not there</u>. It's recommended that you do your own costing based on this model, plugging in your own numbers to see where you fit.

<u>Utilities (Gas/Electricity/Internet/Cable TV/Water)</u> will average another $300-$400 per month on average. I've used $300 as a working average. Telephone, Internet and cable TV service may be purchased seasonally (November through May), but check to make sure as this may vary from city to city.

<u>Maid service for a 2,000-square-foot house runs $75</u> every two weeks, or $150 per month. Double that for a 4,000-square-foot house.

<u>A gardener will charge $85-$100 per month</u> for a 2,000-square-foot house and double for a 4,000-square foot house, depending, of course, on the amount of landscaping.

If you have a pool, its maintenance will set you back another $100 per month.

Thus, Upper-middle house in a Coachella Valley gated community could hypothetically cost:

HOA/golf/utilities/property tax $3,000 monthly plus

Housekeeper...................................$300
Gardener.................................... $200
Pool...$100
    Grand total: $3,600

Conclusion: to operate your upper-middle home in the desert, Budget **$4K monthly**

55+ Communities

Introduction

Houses priced $200,000 to $800,000

In general, 55+ communities offer free-standing homes ranging from 1,200 to 3,000 square feet costing from $200K to $800K. A single contractor builds the tract houses, or the pre-manufactured home is assembled on site. Houses will be located close together, and most will contain two bedrooms and a den, with only the largest models offering three bedrooms. Some homes may have attached casitas.

Despite HOA dues that tend to stay under $300 monthly, there's more activity inside a 55+ community than at most non-age-restricted gated communities, and usually at no extra cost. In fact, without exception, the 55+ developments we rate offer considerably more activities and facilities than even high-end communities, but without the concierge, stone walkways, French chefs, free cookies, etc.

At 55+ places, residents launch plays, conduct their own golf and tennis tournaments, invite guest speakers and entertainers and create special-interest clubs that generate considerable socialization. Multi-millionaires mix with blue-collar retirees living on fat pensions plus impecunious others inhabiting small homes and getting by on $25K to $35K a year. As many as half of 55+Community residents may own one or more additional homes, living in their 55+ home only during winter months.

Date Palm Country Club

36-200 Date Palm Drive

Cathedral City, CA 92234

760-328-6514

This may be the least expensive 55+ community in the Coachella Valley. Opened in 1971, its manufactured homes cluster around an 18-hole 'executive' par 58, 3,100 yard course. There's a pro shop and restaurant. Of the 538 home sites, all but five or six are filled. Residents n enjoy tennis, shuffleboard and bocce ball, a sauna, whirlpool and spa. Home prices range from $25K to $125K. A perusal of Redfin Date Palm CC real estate offerings show homes for sale for $19K with $1,100 monthly HOA and a 2,100 square foot three-bedroom manufactured home for sale for $414K with an HOA of $130. I also saw homes in this community listed with no HOA, so make sure you inquire.

Heritage Palms

44-291 South Heritage Palms Dr.
Indio, CA 92201
(760) 772-5755

Residences here sell from the $200K to $600K. The community appears tight knit and satisfied. Despite having 1,004 homes,

you won't find the variety of activities available at bigger 55+ developments. Built from 1995 to 2004, the monthly HOA has crept above $300, higher than competitors. Heritage Palms' facilities are first rate. Heritage Palms reportedly suffers from 'age creep.' This means that older members who've died off or moved away aren't being replaced in enough numbers by the 55-65 age cohort. Does this suggest future trouble? Hopefully not. Heritage Palms is a pleasant, sociable community whose residents almost uniformly rate it highly. The housing is similar to the two Del Webb Sun Cities and Trilogy, meaning it is well built for desert heat. Homes here can be purchased for slightly less for equivalent square footage than at Sun City or Shadow Hills, although this depends on the house, its location within the complex, its views, closeness to

the clubhouse and other factors.

Hovnanian Four Seasons Palm Springs

1800 Sand Canyon
Palm Springs, CA 92262
(866)-347-7116 or (888)-287-2490

This 2,825 square foot Hovnanian Palm Springs home can be purchased for between $340- and $375K, a lot of square footage for the money.

This community has 477 freestanding homes scaled from 1,900 to 2,800 square feet, priced from $200,000 to the high $300,000s, built from 2006 to 2010 and located five miles north of Palm Springs. HOAs average $275 monthly. There's no golf course or indoor pool. The clubhouse includes an exercise room, salon, café, ballroom and hobby rooms for arts and crafts, plus an outside Olympic-size pool, tennis, pickle ball, bocce ball and shuffleboard courts. Golf options include the Palm Springs Country Club Golf

Course, which dates to the 1960's and isn't all that much fun. Complaints about construction sloppiness have surfaced on Yelp. Such complaints resonate. I once looked at a Hovnanian 55+ development in Bakersfield, California and noticed crooked joints and other problems, and these were in the model homes! So if you buy here, thoroughly eyeball any house you're considering.

Hovnanian Four Seasons Terra Lago

8400 Terra Lago Parkway
Indio, CA 92203
(888) 631-1006
www.khov4seasons.com/4-seasons-terra-lago

This 635-home community broke ground in 2015. You seemingly drive forever to enter or exit it. Model homes and the clubhouse are already open. As of Winter, 2015, no tennis courts have been built. There will be no golf course. Homes resemble those of Sun City Shadow Hills and Sun City Palm Desert and duplicate the 1,200-3,000 square-foot sizing and $200,000 to high $400,000 pricing. Hovnanian adroitly purchased a bankrupt contractor's

This 1,500sf home is offered for $302K but figure a minimum of $30K in upgrades to get it the way you want

land facing the unaffiliated Terra Lago Club golf course. Hovnanian residents can join this club for a reduced fee. Other than golf course frontage, the land is boring flat and the community will be small, which in 55+ communities is not good, meaning corralling enough residents to populate a rich diversity of clubs and activities will be difficult if not impossible.

Depiction of Terra Lago clubhouse.

Hovnanian Four Seasons Terra Lago's monthly HOA will start at $202 monthly, which for the moment twill be the Desert's lowest. Not having a golf course (They always run a deficit) should help keep the HOA low.

Ivey Ranch Country Club

74580 Varner Road, Thousand Palms, CA 92276
(760)-343-2013
iveyranchgolf.com

This 395-manufactured home community sits across the 10
Freeway from Palm Desert and Rancho Mirage and is accessed by

Varner Road from either Cook Street or Washington Boulevard.
The community has its own clubhouse, restaurant, work-out room,
four pools, two spas and a nine-hole golf course. A $400 pass lets
you play there all year long. The Community is gated with full-
time

guard and surprisingly well maintained when you consider HOA monthly dues are only $220. Prices range from repossess homes costing $75K to $150K, although on one realtor's site I saw one

beautifully upgraded unit selling for over $200K. This is the least expensive 55+ golf community I've found and if money is tight, you should give it a look. The only downside —bank repossessions of which thee are many.

Palm Desert Greens
73-750 Country Club Drive
Palm Desert, CA 92260
(760) 346-8005
http://www.pdgcc.com

Built in the early to mid 1970's, this development includes 1,922 manufactured/mobile homes. They range from 1,300 to 1,800 square feet and cost $80K to $140K. Many homes face the community's 18-hole golf course, which features four small lakes. Other amenities: seven tennis courts, three outdoor pools, a sauna, steam room, shuffleboard, picnic areas, fitness center, restaurant and numerous resident-initiated clubs. The monthly HOA runs $260, which includes free golf. The community is located off Country Club Road cheek to jowl with more expensive communities. I recently met a couple from Palm Desert Greens. They'd found the 55+ Sun City Palm Desert gated community too expensive and too big, they said.

"Palm Desert Greens has the same stuff," they said. What's different in the typical 1400 square foot Palm Desert Greens home? You won't have a private enclosed green space 'out back' where you can relax without being eyed. You'll also make do with a carport instead of a garage and other manufactured housing within three feet of your property line. Still, the amenities, the price of a Palm Desert Greens home and the low monthly HOA

may make this community the Desert's best bargain.

Sun City Palm Desert

38180 Del Webb Blvd
Palm Desert, CA 92211
(760)-200-210
scpdca.com

This is the Big Kahuna of 55+ gated communities—1,600 acres big. The main clubhouse is cavernous and reminds you of a government building. On premise are 5,000+ tract houses priced from $220,000 to $700,000 and sized from 1,000 to 3300 square feet. As many as nine thousand people live here in season. The amenities equal or outdo its competition, to include two well-maintained golf courses plus first- class pickle ball and tennis facilities. There's even a softball league composed entirely of residents. Sun City Palm

Desert is self-managed and residents pay their 270 monthly HOA fee regardless of their home's square footage. Sun City Palm Desert has been around since early 1992 and by 2003 had sold out. There are sidewalks (not typical of most desert gated communities), multiple clubhouses, lending libraries and a fun pizza place run by an outside firm. Otherwise, food options are so-so. The size of the place breeds a sense of individual isolation, but that may be just my imagination. There's plenty to do and over

70 clubs, classes and lectures for personal enrichment. You don't get servants dressed like Swiss Army guards or a clubhouse and bar attached to men's or women's locker rooms, but you do get a plethora of fun community activities. and superb facilities in which to pursue them. There's even an on-site post office.

Sun City Shadow Hills

80814 Sun City Boulevard

Indio, CA 922203

(760) 345-4349

Groundbreaking began at this gated community in 2004 and sell-out of this 3,400-home community came in March 2016. Like other 55+ communities we cover, houses range from 1,200 to 3,000 square feet and sell for $220,000 to $700,000. Compared to Sun City Palm Desert, also a Del Webb development, SCSH lacks sidewalks but is newer and (arguably) better built with the latest insulation, interior wiring, thermo pane windows, etc. It also sits in the Imperial Electric District, meaning electricity is 29% cheaper than Edson, which serves Sun City Palm Desert.SCSH tennis and pick ball facilities offer no drinking fountains between courts, no

pro shop, etc. and are thus below average for 55+ communities, and for some reason the developer built too many bocce ball courts. The main clubhouse effuses a slightly 'old maid' aesthetic. The newer clubhouse in the third and final build-out phase is better done and smaller. It has an indoor walking/running track. The HOA, $217, is the Valley's lowest for any Valley 55+ community. The number of clubs/activities either ranks among the best or is the best. There are the Friday Night movies with free popcorn. Once a month, LA comics put on a show to sold-out audiences. SCSH

The Sun City Shadow Hills exercise area overlooks a golf course and mountains.

residents skew about a decade younger on average than residents of Sun City Palm Desert and Heritage Palms. In 2016, six new pickle ball courts were added and the pool area behind its second club house expanded. SCSH's two gym sand indoor pool remain, 12 years after its founding, state-of-the-art.

Suncrest

73-450 Country Club Drive
Palm Desert, CA 92260
(760) 340-2467
(No Internet address)

This mobile and manufactured home community opened in 1980, has three community pools, a clubhouse with billiard room, lounge, library, café open at lunch, dance floor and a desk that serves as a golf pro shop. It has three lighted tennis courts, BBQ areas and a nine-hole golf course that costs $25 to play, presumably one of the cheapest or the cheapest all-year rate in the Coachella Valley. Housing runs $30K to $150K. There are no HOA dues. Instead,This 1,760 square foot manufactured home in Suncrest sold for $90K after only five days on the market.

depending on location, residents pay to rent their property for between $650 to $850 per month. Most homes offer approximately 1,400 square feet but some run as big as 2,300 square feet. Individual houses have carports but no private land. There are bargains at Suncrest. I have a friend who bought a 1,400 square

Suncrest's clubhouse

foot manufactured home there for $25,000, put $15K into it, to include granite countertops and stainless steel appliances and now believes he could get $75K but doesn't want to sell."I'm across the street from a big shopping center," he said, "and ten minutes drive to El Paseo. My living costs have become almost embarrassingly low. I'm staying put."

Trilogy at La Quinta

60-151 Trilogy Parkway

La Quinta, CA 92253

(760) 777-6059

The 1,238 houses in this 536-acre development are comparable to Sun City Shadow Hills, meaning they are newer (2006-2012), wired for cable, with double-pane windows and the latest insulation. House sizes range from 1,381 to 2,769 square feet and are priced similarly as well ($200,000 to $700,000). Trilogy offers what other 55+ communities provide plus a spa where you can get massages, waxing and other body treatments. The problem with Trilogy: It's stuck way the hell at the end of Jefferson

Avenue near nothing. Getting a diet Coke, milk or a pizza means a 20-minute trek each way. Also, Trilogy's relatively small population doesn't comprise a big enough nucleus to create the variety of clubs and activities that make other 55+ developments so attractive. This is not to say Trilogy isn't a well thought out community. It is.It has indoor and outdoor pools and beautifully landscaped surroundings and prices recently have eased, making it a more attractive proposition. HOA dues are currently $288 monthly. Unlike 55+ communities in the desert who own their own golf courses, Trilogy no longer does. The course is now privately owned and charges $12K for a single and $17K for a couple to join. If you don't have your own golf cart, add an additional $500 annually. How does this sit with members who bought in Trilogy thinking they'd be able to play their own course? I doubt they're pleased.

Trilogy at the Polo Club

51682 Hawthorne Court

Indio, CA 92201

(800) 685-6494

http://www.trilogylife.com/communities/california/polo

As of February 2016, this development remains under construction. The new clubhouse has opened There will be no golf course. Sample houses have been built and sales are well underway. These sample houses have solar built into the price, but once they're sold it's not guaranteed subsequent houses will include solar other than as an extra-charge item. Many Trilogy Polo Club model homes feature walls of sliding glass, which architects have used to seemingly

This 2,205 square foot 'Imaginare' is offered for $419K. Figure another $30-50K to add solar and other upgrades. Check the site, as discounts are frequently offered.

expand a home's square footage. You pay a lot extra for this. Prices are approximately 15% higher than equivalently sized homes in Del Webb's Sun City Palm Desert or Sun City Shadow Hills. Whether the marketplace will accept such pricing remains to be seen. There's nothing special about the complex's layout or amenities and it abuts a downscale community. At build-out, no more than 750 homes are planned, suggesting this community will experience the same problem faced by Heritage Palms and Trilogy La Quinta —not enough residents to populate tennis,

crafts and other clubs. Prices start in the high $200Ks and go to $800K, but these are bare-bones homes. Figure on spending an additional minimum of $30- to $50K more. The HOA is temporarily set at $300 monthly, exceptionally high considering there's no golf course.

Villa Portafino

4001 Via Portofino

Palm Desert, CA 92260

The Portofino clubhouse

A lot has happened to this community in the past year. Launched

in the early 2000's, its builder went bankrupt in 2007. His concept: build elegant small apartment homes using finishes and appointments typical of much higher priced condominiums and put them on the market for $300K to $400K, plus include a luxuriously appointed clubhouse with movie theater, restaurant, pub, library, meeting rooms, pool table and game rooms. The clubhouse got built as did maybe a third of the homes before the bankruptcy. When Villa Portafino re-opened under new ownership four years later, these homes, ranging from 1,200 to 1,500 square feet sold quickly for $250K. Buyers seemed not to notice that none of them included garages or that ground-level condos had patios that opened on to the street or faced another building. The new owner is now building new condos. These have narrow garages, meaning you can't park a car next to a golf car or another car. You have to park one behind the other. Now under construction: duplexes, triplexes and free standing homes ranging from $330K to $500K. There's a pool outside the clubhouse with a lovely view of the mountains but no golf course and no tennis or bocce ball courts. Apparently, the market is for over-55-ers who choose not to exercise. This suggests the owner is seeking an older clientele. HOA dues, at $375 per month, are high for a club without a golf course, although this fee includes pest control, window washing, building insurance, cable TV, water and trash service. Some newly built homes also include solar and all homes are wired for it. In the main clubhouse there's what looks like a spare room sparsely occupied by a few work-out machines. The dining room is beautiful. I haven't eat in it but the menu looks good and residents I talked with said the food is as well.

Summary

Communities that restrict home sales to those 55+ can seem similar to the mid-priced desert gated communities described in the next section, and in many respects they are.

Home owners in both developments tend not to be rich but certainly not poor, the only clear difference being; the desert's mid-priced communities include people of all ages. If a couple buys a house in a 55+ development, one of them must be 55 or older.

Desert 55+ communities generally offer more amenities than bargain-priced developments, to include indoor as well as outdoor pools, two golf courses instead of one, and HOAs under $300 monthly, which mid-priced communities typically don't come close to matching.

Visiting teenagers' and young children's use of amenities may be restricted or heavily monitored. Fire trucks and ambulances visit more often because older people get sick.

The size of some 55+communities such as Del Webb Sun City Palm Desert support upwards of 10,000 residents during high season November through April. Most mid-priced communities support maybe 1/5th of that.

So why choose a 55+ community?

Cost is the major reason. If you can afford a high-end community's yearly $70K+ household maintenance costs, you'll enjoy an on-premise masseuse and a concierge to do your shopping.

You'll walk into your gym's locker room where an attendant will hand you a towel. You'll socialize in a small, uncrowded, exclusive community, experience beautifully outfitted clubhouses, live in a custom-built five- and six-thousand square foot home.

You'll have privacy and enjoy the companionship of other ultra rich people who treat you as an ordinary   person and friend and not a god.

I know of an anecdotal instance when someone may have chosen a 55+ community over a high-end one. A Vancouver couple bought an entire cul de sac's 2,700 square-foot, $625K-plus homes inside Sun City Shadow Hills, gifting one home to each of their four children and keeping one for themselves.

Conclusion: The Desert's 55+ communities include their share   of multi-millionaires, but the vast majority of residents are 'comfortable' middle class.

What about differences between 55+ communities?

The two Del Webb Sun City communities dominate the 55+ group. Trilogy has priced its homes higher while building smaller more intimate communities and until recently, its buyers paid a premium; but recentlyTrilogy's prices have dropped to the level of the Del Webb communities for equivalently sized homes. Until more retail development happens, Trilogy's location at the far and desolate end of Jefferson Avenue remains problematic. Both Trilogy and the Hovnanian developments solve the golf course deficit 'problem' by doing away with it. This may work to help keep their HOAs lower but so far it has not. Their

HOAs remain higher than those at either Pulte/Del Webb development. Hovnanian in the past has been plagued with 'quality' issues. I looked for shoddy workmanship in the Hovnanian Terra Lago development and found none, suggesting that the developer has learned some lessons in that regard. As for Heritage Palms, you couldn't find a nicer community, but like

Trilogy in La Quinta it charges its residents an annual multiple $K fee to play golf, effectively pricing their 55+ experience higher than the Del Webb communities without providing more for the dollar. Of the two Del Webb developments, the Shadow Hills community skews younger but the older Palm Desert community has better done amenities.

Del Webb Palm Desert housing prices trend slightly higher than Shadow Hills for an equivalently sized house. Conventional wisdom says that now that Shadow Hills has sold out, housing prices in both communities should more closely approximate each other. Maybe so. We'll see.

It's rumored that Del Webb/Pulte has bought land near the Aqua Caliente Casino in Rancho Mirage for a community minus golf course, joining Trilogy, Villa Portafino and Hovnanian in pursuit of that strategy. As of March, 2016, progress on this site is being stalled by zoning and other issues.

As for Portofino, it lacks a golf course, tennis courts, bocce ball and pickle ball, and has the highest HOAs of all, suggesting its market is for older-than-55+'ers. Manufactured housing 55+ communities, Suncrest, Ivey Ranch, Date Palm and Palm Desert Greens would be placed in the 'bargain-priced' section of this book were they open for adults of all ages. Their home resale prices place them there. This is not to denigrate either community. They provide a lot of amenities for the price

COMPARISON CHART
55+ Gated Communities

Club Homes	City	Monthly Golf Price	Golf Debut	HOA	Fee	Dues	
Date Palm	Cathedral City	$75K	1969	$125	None	None	528
Her. Palms	Indio	$175K	1995	$295	None	$267	1,004
Hovnanan PS	Palm Springs	$325K	2002	$278	None	None	477
Hovnanian TL	Indio	$350K	1914	$202	None	None	635
Ivey Ranch	Thousand Palms	$100K	1985	$280	$400	None	395
Palm Desert Greens	Palm Desert	$100K	1975	$265	None	None	1,850
Sun Cty PD	Palm Desert	$400K	1992	$228	None	None	4,949
SunCty SH	Indio	$375K	2004	$217	None	None	3,400
Suncrest	Palm Desert	$50K	1980	$600	None	None	360
Trilogy LA	La Quinta	$400K	2004	$288	None	None	1,238
Trilogy Polo	La Quinta	$400K	2014	$300	None	None	800
Villa Porto.	Palm Desert	$275K	2005	#375	None	None	460

55+ Communities
Estimated monthly housing expense

Community	HOA/golf	Utilities	Prop Tax+	Total
Heritage Palms	$562	$300	$350	$1,212
Portofino	#375	$300	$350	$1,025
Suncrest	$600	$300	$75	$975
Trilogy Polo Club	$300	$300	$350	$950
Trilogy La Quinta	$288	$300	$350	$938
Hovnanian Palm Springs	$278	$300	$350	$928
Sun City Palm Desert	$270	$300	$350	$920

Average: $951

Community	HOA/golf	Utilities	Prop Tax+	Total
Palm Desert Greens	$265	$300	$350	$915
Sun City Shadow Hills	$217	$300	$350	$867
Hovnanian Terra Lago	$202	$300	$350	$857
Ivey Ranch	$220	$300	$100	$660
Date Palm	$125	$300	$75	$600

Notes

1.2% of a home assessed at $350K equals $350 per month.

$ amounts show fixed on-going monthly expenses <u>even if you're not there</u>. It's recommended that you plug in your own numbers to see where you fit on the continuum shown above. I've used $300 as a working average for all utilities, to include Cable TV and Internet. Telephone, Internet and cable TV service may be purchased seasonally (November through May), but check to make sure as this may vary from city to city.

<u>Maid service for a 2,000-square-foot house runs $75</u> every two weeks, or $150 per month.

<u>A gardener will charge $85-$100 per month</u> for a 2,000-square-foot house, depending, of course, on the amount of landscaping.

<u>If you have a pool, its maintenance will set you back another $100 per month</u>.

Thus, owning a 55+ home in a Coachella Valley gated community, could hypothetically cost:

HOA/golf/utilities/property tax...................$950 monthly
Housekeeper....................................... $150   "
        Gardener... ....$85   "
           Pool...$100
"   Grand total: $1,285
"

Conclusion: Budget **$1,400 monthly** to operate your 55+ home in the desert.

Mid-priced Communities

Introduction

Houses priced $200K to $499,000K+

NOTE: Statistics are taken from the public domain, realtor and gated community websites and conversations with gated community GM's and HOA personnel. The author has made every effort to include the latest and most accurate figures. If you spot an error, email me at jbarnes3609@gmail.com.

Mid-priced Communities tend to be as much as 40 years old, the houses packed close together with less personal service than High-end and Upper-middle venues deliver. There may not be spa services but the usual amenities –golf, tennis, clubhouse, restaurant, etc., — will all be there.

The majority of mid-priced communities struggle finding new members. This may be due to their relative lack of prestige, the growing unpopularity of golf among younger population subsets, plus competition from newer and more amenity-rich 55+ communities.

I found several of these mid-priced communities featured on, Expedia.com, Tripadvisor.com and other travel sites, a tip-off that many of these developments are filled with rental units. You need to ask yourself if that's the kind of 'country club' experience you seek.

Avondale Country Club

75-300 Avondale Drive

Palm Desert, CA 92211

(760) -345-2727

avondalegolfclub.com

This gated community is borderline Upper-middle and the only reason it isn't placed there is its relative lack of $1M properties, although it does have a few. The 'sweet spot' in this community is a home price of between $400- and $800K. This club is one of the Desert's longest lasting gated communities, tracing its origins back to 1969. Its golf initiation fee is $5K for non-residents. If you buy a home in Avondale, that fee is waved. Non-resident golfers pay annual dues of $10,473. Residents pay $9,728. Both residents and

non-residents must spend a minimum of $1,100 annually on food, another $150 in the golf shop and an additional $200 annually for range fees. Plus there are additional cart and other costs.
Avondale has 305 single-family attached and detached residences featuring two to seven bedrooms ranging from 1,632 to over 4000 square feet, almost all built from the early 1970's through 2000 by different builders, so you don't get a Tuscan or Spanish theme dominating. There's no spa, no athletic club and only one tennis court. HOA monthlies are $363. That also entitles you to a full Social Membership, which includes clubhouse use and 12 golf rounds per household, not enough for avid golfers but a nice extra.

Avondale golf course lake view.

Bermuda Dunes CC

42360 Adams Street

Bermuda Dunes, CA 92203

(760) 345-2771

Twenty years ago, this gated community would fit in the high-end category. Established in 1959, it's the Coachella Valley's oldest continuing golf venue and once. a long time ago hosted the Bob

Hope Classic PGA tournament. Clark Gable and Eddie Fisher were original homeowners. People of similar fame or notoriety don't own here now. Housing styles vary by decade and builder. This creates a somewhat disjointed esthetic. Most homes are old with unwashed exteriors that create a shopworn appearance. There are some spectacularly big and opulent places on premise, but much of the architecture seems to this viewer both dated and of questionable taste. You'll drive by a huge house and see a leaning, rusted mail box stuck in the ground in front. HOAs average $500+ monthly. All homes front or back the golf course. Seventeen different homeowner associations are represented. Some, such as Bellissimo and

Castle Harbor are gated inside the Bermuda Dunes Country Club gates. In all, Bermuda Dunes has 1,200 homes, making it one of the Coachella Valley's larger golf club communities. Golf membership initiation costs $10K. Monthly dues start at $299 for an individual age 21-35, $544 for someone 46-54 and $848

Bermuda Dunes Country Club Dining Room

monthly for everyone else. The club recently began offering 'free' golf memberships to new Trilogy at the Polo Club home purchasers. Either Bermuda Dunes Golf Club or Trilogy is absorbing the initiation fee or maybe they split the cost. In November 2015, the club offered anyone a chance to play for $595 per month for a single and $695 for a   family with no initiation fee. In February 2016 I checked again. This special is still offered. On real estate websites you'll see a lot of big and impressive Bermuda Dunes CC estates for sale, many on the market for half a year or longer with multiple price reductions.

Vibrante
760-289-9078

At the Jefferson Avenue-facing wall inside the Bermuda Dunes Country Club sit 12 new single-story homes built by Corman Leigh Homes of Temecula, Ca. They range from 2,828 to 3,002 square feet with prices starting in the high $400Ks. Each offers energy efficiencies, three- bay garages, recessed lighting, choice of flooring, stainless steel kitchens with marble surfaces and something called Piedrafina bathroom surfaces. Piedrafina is leftover marble crushed with resin into flat surfaces. Not sure this is an improvement over actual marble and strongly suspect it is cheaper. I've had a look at these homes. They're nice but nothing special. The proposed HOA will be $151 per month with another $121 yearly charge for cable TV. $25K in incentives are offered, most involving upgrades. These incentives will probably remain until all the homes are sold. Residents get access to the Bermuda Dunes Country Club amenities for a price, which at publication date was not yet available.

Chaparral Country Club
100 Chaparral Drive
Palm Desert CA 92260
(760) 340-1893

Open for the first time in 1979, Chaparral offers residents a small clubhouse, 21 pools and no spa. Six-hundred-and-twenty-five attached condos surround the golf course. Construction of a 4,800 square foot, multi-purpose building to house a gym, card and crafts room, meeting room, restrooms and spa was recently completed. You'll find teaching pros for golf and tennis but only three tennis courts. Chaparral management touts the club's fiscal discipline and its $1M-plus reserves, a good sign. As for social activities, there don't appear to be many. The web site mentions card games and a book club, which suggests a membership on the old side. Nothing wrong with that; but country clubs like Chaparral can't survive without new blood. Houses and condos here run from 1600 to 3,245 square feet. The 2015 median sale price was $ 309K. The monthly HOA is $460. Golf costs $126 per month for one person and $155 per month for a couple. The $7.5K golf initiation fee is payable in three installments. Every resident pays $252.30 monthly for a Social Membership and must spend at least $675 annually on food and beverages. According to one realtor site, approximately 23% of Chaparral's homes were for sale as of late January 2016. There also seems to be a sizable rental market for these homes, suggesting a large absentee-owner base. I'd be careful before investing here.

View of Chaparral golf-view homes.

Desert Falls Country Club
1111 Desert Falls Parkway
Palm Desert, CA 92211
(760) 340-5646

ClubCorp operates golf resorts all over the United States to include
Mission Hills and Indian Wells country clubs and Desert Falls here
in the Coachella Valley. Pay a $1,500 initiation fee to Desert Falls
and you get reciprocal Golf and Social privileges at more than 200
private clubs and 700 hotels and resorts across the country.
Founded in 1984, Desert Falls has 1,100 upper- and lower-story

condos sized from 1,300 to 2,300 square feet costing from the low
$200Ks to around $450K with most units priced from the high
$100Ks to the mid-$300Ks.The monthly HOA is $470, but may be
higher or lower depending on the unit. Approximately 10% of the
units are for rent. The emphasis is on golf, to include a three-
tiered driving range and nine-hole putting green in addition to an
18-hole course. The rental situation will likely get worse as more
members die off. Hopefully, owner ClubCorp has deep pockets and
will keep this gated community relevant.

The Estates at Desert falls, a 23-home enclave located within Desert Falls Country Club has homes selling for $1M to $1.35M, with a monthly HOA of $393. Owners can use Desert Falls'

amenities.

Indian Springs

79940 Westward Ho Drive
Indio, CA 92201
(760) 200-8988
http://www.indianspringsgc.com

Indian Springs opened in 1962 but almost all its 709 homes were built from 2001 to 2005. This development's golf course recently changed hands. Vancouver native Ken Hanna bought it and its clubhouse and lives there in a home facing the sixth tee. He wants to turn the restaurant into a popular public sit-down place, arguing that 900 Indio and La Quinta residences are "within a chip shot" of the club and course. Whether the golf courses and course and

restaurant will become long-term moneymakers for Mr. Hanna remains to be seen. The golf course is open to the public and completely redone in 2000. Annual golf passes go for $5K for individuals and $7,500 for families. Sources tell me that discounts are available. Check to see. Houses range from 1,529 to 2,716 square feet with up to four bedrooms and a three-car garage. Home prices run $250K to $500K. HOA dues are $266 monthly. Hundreds of renters and day players use the golf course, which can be played for under $100. Anyone thinking of buying in Indian Springs should check this gated community's finances and its percentage of rentals. If rentals equal or surpass 20% of total residences, then beware.

The Lakes

161 Old Ranch Road
Palm Desert, CA 92211
(760)568-4321
http://www.thelakescc.com

The Lakes is filled with rivers, rocky rills and lakes with stone

pathways leading everywhere. You won't find a crack or piece of errant stone anywhere. Lounge areas offer free coffee. The food in the Santa Fe Grill, its bar and the clubhouse Mountain View Room is well above average. There are golf and tennis pro shops, plus mint gargle and sunscreen in bathrooms. The golf course is exclusively for members, meaning few outsiders, which makes tee times easier to get. By almost any measure, The Lakes, were it not for its relatively low home prices, would be placed in the Upper-middle category. Alas, we're talking about a condo-only community with

$1,100 monthly HOA for a non-golf household and $1,645 for a golf membership, plus a $10K one-time initiation fee. Noted: The Lakes' $1,100 monthly golf dues include use of all facilities, but still, these costs are uncomfortably high for the mid-priced category. This year, recycled water for the first time is employed exclusively for the lakes and nine of the 18 holes, with the

One of the many lakes residents enjoy.

remaining holes to be converted in 2016. In the past four years, the clubhouse, roads, tennis center and all pools have been updated. The Lakes now has a reserve fund it adds to yearly, although at present it is only approximately one-third of what it needs to be. Housing runs $160K to $700K, with the average unit falling in the $250K to $350K range.

Lake Mirage Racquet Club

72727 Country Club Drive

Rancho Mirage, CA

760-773-3522

This club relies on realtor websites and no longer has its own, which is not to diminish it. The community features a 13-acre lake in the middle of 25 acres of bike paths, nine tennis courts, a three-hole pitch 'n' putt, 10 swimming

pools/spas and plenty of rentals at $120 to $140 per night. The rentals are a red flag in what is otherwise an attractive story. In addition, the HOA is high --$672 monthly. On the 'plus' side, many home sites have their own docks, so you can kayak on the lake and visit neighbors that way. Housing ranges from 1,600 to 3,000 square feet and re-sales have been running $250K to $400K. In addition to the lake, there's a small clubhouse with outdoor barbecue, billiards room, fitness center, tennis courts and meeting rooms. Regardless of size, these 'townhouses' are actually condos, meaning that roofs, water systems, etc. have to be repaired not by the individual home owner but simultaneously by the HOA association for every home. I've not been able to determine the size of this community's reserve fund, but if you plan to buy here, you should check. Lakes mean leaks, ground erosion and other problems. Also, the cost of keeping the lake full weighs heavy on homeowners now that drought water

restrictions are in play. Plus the community is dotted with pools rather than one single community pool attached to the clubhouse. This also suggests added maintenance expense.

Marrakesh Country Club
47000 Marrakesh Drive, Palm Desert, Ca 92260
(760) 568-2268
www.marrakeshcountryclub.com

Marrakesh has been getting some good vibes lately that have helped increase selling prices of its mid-century homes. Founded in 1968 on 154 acres, the Club was designed with 364 residences not crowded cheek-to-jowl like similar developments. All face a par-60 executive course that can be played in three hours or less. Marrakesh's distinctive rose-sandstone colored walls and building architecture is called 'Hollywood Regency,' which references mid-century modern,

, which references Bauhaus, which means a minimum of decorative touches and the belief that 'less is more.' This you will find at

Marrakesh, along with floor-to-ceiling windows that let the outside in. Marrakesh's 364 homes are broken into individual complexes each with 24 homes grouped around 14 pools. A golf membership costs $15K with $200 monthly dues, a Social membership $230 monthly. Resident average age is likely high. Homes run from 2000 to 3,000 square feet. The HOAs, and there are two, total an exceptionally high $905 per month. House prices run from the high $200Ks to the high $300Ks. Amenities are not equal to newer competition, although Marrakesh's architecture gives it a uniqueness most complexes lack. This gated complex is often included on mid-century home tours offered 'in season' every year. Despite its relative lack of amenities and high HOA monthly dues, its architectural uniqueness and charm have kept it relevant.

Marrakesh contains an abundance of old palms like these.

Monterey Country Club

41-500 Monterey Avenue
Palm Desert, CA 92260
(760) 568-9311

The moment you pass through the gates of this 1,206-home community you'll know it's been around awhile, meaning since 1979. That's not to say Monterey isn't well maintained. It is. A golf membership costs $7K with monthly golf dues $615 for a family. If you're contemplating buying a home at Monterey, specials are available. Condo prices range from $200K to $400K sized from 1,300 to 2,600 SF. The monthly HOA runs $480 plus $100 for Social/Fitness dues. Both tennis and golf facilities are above average for mid-priced gated communities. There are 19 tennis courts, ten lighted, plus a sunken stadium court, a separate tennis clubhouse, swimming pool, a full driving range for golfers plus a short-game practice area and putting green. You can play on two-and-a-half golf courses and in season (November to May) there's a full range of social activities inside the clubhouse and at various nearby venues but not so much the rest of the year. Typical of older clubs, there are lots and lots of rentals. Monterey strikes me as a 'middle of the road' place, meaning you won't be wowed but will find the right kinds of amenities and a pleasant enough resort experience.t enough resort experience.

Sunset at Monterey.

Oasis Country Club

43-300 Casbah Way
Palm Desert, CA 92260
(760) 200-0522
https://www.theoasiscountryclub.com

Incorporated in 1983, this condo community contains 746 one- and two-story residences, some attached and others freestanding. Homes range from 775 to 1,803 square feet for a three-bedroom unit. The monthly HOA is $532. Home values stretch from the mid 100Ks to $300K+ with the 'sweet spot' around $250K. Twenty-one community pools, 20 jacuzzis and 22 lakes dot the property. There are 12 tennis courts, three of them clay, and three pickle ball courts. The 18-hole golf course is public but members get tee-time priority. A golf membership costs $3.2k plus $3K annual dues, or you can pay as you play. Overall, the Oasis strikes me as less than fancy (other than the entrance), with no glaring negatives other than the number of rental units, which may be nearing a 'tipping point.' I have no idea what this tipping point might be, but a good guess would be when 25% or more residences cross over. Recently, this community has been doing some impressive advertising on social media, either suggesting it's not about to 'fold its tent' if membership doesn't start to grow.

Omni Rancho Las Palmas

42001 Rancho Mirage, CA
(760) 837-9631
www.omnirancholaspalmas.com

Bob Hope Drive Rancho Las Palmas is both a public resort and a private country club. Omni Hotels & Resorts Corporation owns the land, clubhouse and golf course. Condo owners own their homes and support their own independent HOA. There are advantages to such an arrangement. True, forming a friendly, interactive community is difficult with renters and vacationers moving in and out daily. On the other hand, a giant corporation's ownership can bring long- haul stability. Plus there's funding for tennis pros, swimming coaches, a water park called Splashtopia with its own ambling, ratable river, a 100-foot water slide, Jacuzzi, sandy beach, fountains and sprinklers for kids to run through and the golf course, all of which tend to lose money in the typical gated community. Also, Omni's consistent vacationer rental income helps hold down HOA fees for permanent owners. Asking prices for the condos, most of them sized 1,200 to

2,200 square feet and built between 1977 and '78 range from $250K to $475K. HOA's are $475 to $600 monthly based on square footage. Two golf memberships are offered –the first being the Signature, which features zero initiation fee and homeowner annual dues of $6.75K for a family and $4.925K for a single person. If you don't live in the community, an annual Family Plan costs $7.5K and a single membership $5.660K. There's also a 'Junior' annual plan for$4.925 if you're under 50 years of age. Tennis memberships run $995 annually for a single and $1595 for a full family.

Outdoor Resort Indio
80-394 Avenue 48
Indio, A 92201
800-892-2992

The above photo of this gated resort exclusively for Class A Motor coaches only doesn't do this community justice. Opened in 2003, Outdoor Resort Indio, a sister development with Outdoor Resort

Palm Springs, outdoes its sibling with 419 better positioned lots and more amenities. zumba and pilates workouts are available, as are water aerobics, lawn bowling, dance lessons, a theatrical group, motorcycle riding club, bible study, yoga, art classes, a book club and likely anything else you can imagine. Six new pickle ball courts were added in the past year, there's tennis and an 18-hole, par-three golf course. If you're interested in buying here, lots facing the golf course sell from $58K to $395K. Privacy lots not facing the course run anywhere from $34K to $115K. The more expensive lots come with built-in dining areas, pergola, large outdoor kitchen with dual electric ranges, fireplaces, TV, bar/ refrigerator and a circular approach driveway plus golf course and mountain view. There's a clubhouse, work-out room, spa, pools and formal dining room. Thirty-seven lots changed hands

in 2015 and already in January 2016 19 lots found new owners. You can only buy or rent if you drive a Class A Motor coach. No trucks pulling campers behind them are accepted. I played here with my club's pickle ball team in 2015 and was impressed with the facilities and the people. This RV resort represents the best there is in the Coachella Valley and maybe in all of America.

Palm Desert Tennis Club

48240 Racquet Lane

Palm Desert, CA

(760) 346-5683

palmdeserttennisclub.com

This gated community was founded in 1973. U.S. Open champion Tony Trabert was once a member. Its100 homes and eight night-lit tennis courts sit on just 20 acres.The clubhouse is small but big enough to host events for the tightly knit community.You'll find a lounge, billiard room, lending library, bathrooms and a kitchen. Many of the 100 three-bedroom condominiums are small and

haven't been updated, meaning deals can be had.They average 1,500 square feet with a few at 1,742 square feet. Prices run in the low to mid $200K's and have been stagnant or falling. A family membership costs $1,307 and a single membership $1050. Non residents also can pay this fee and take advantage of the facilities and activities. Some Ironwood Country Club residents from a mile away have done so. There are likely members from other clubs I don't know about who've done the same. The monthly HOA runs

$540, which doesn't get you pickle ball courts, indoor pools or rooms for pottery and other crafts. Palm Desert Tennis Club is strictly for tennis players. Community cohesiveness is palpable. Members bring cookies and cakes to the clubhouse in the mornings and the small kitchen produces lunches and dinners on occasion. There are lots of potluck get-togethers. If someone's sick, neighbors help out. If you're a guest, and I have been, people treat you with utmost courtesy. For anyone seeking a friendly, intimate environment with as much tennis as you want, this is the place, although your fellow residents' old age, a lack of strong 3.5 and above tennis players and worrisome home resale prices make choosing Palm Desert Tennis Club a gamble.

Palm Valley Country Club

76501 Begonia Lane

Palm Desert, CA 92211

(760) 345-2737

Palm Valley is the first club I've encountered that states that its Reserves are 100% funded. Opened in 1983, you'll find only condos here. They run 938 to 2,489 square feet and are priced

from $150K to $700K. The HOA runs $511 monthly and includes Verizon Internet and Cable TV plus HBO and Showtime. In addition, residents pay $118 Social monthly dues to the Palm Valley Golf Club, making total monthly resident fees $629. To access the 16 tennis courts, you'll need a tennis membership, which costs a family an additional $195 monthly for a family and $110 monthly for an individual, which ups costs to $8ll, and there's no golf included in any of that. However, a Platinum membership rolls tennis and golf into one package and costs $689 monthly. Go that route and your total activity payout will be $1,200 monthly. Homeowners pay no golf initiation fee. Golfers get use of two 18-hole private courses plus a full driving range and short game practice area. Both men's and women's locker rooms feature Jacuzzis. Rare for this price point, there's a day spa offering facials, haircuts and massages. There's also a golf and tennis pro shop with special member pricing, two restaurants, a lounge, an Olympic-size pool and an athletic club with cardiovascular and weight training machines. The Palm Valley Golf Club is separate from its residential HOA and owned by the American Golf Association. Pay them an added $350 per year

and you can golf at 25 private country clubs and 125 resorts across America. The tennis and golf groups have their own heavy schedule of events in season as do the two restaurants, which feature pasta nights, Sunday brunches and a variety of themed events (Super Bowl, Valentine's Day, etc.) Unlike most desert clubs, Palm Valley has a lot of events scheduled for children. Palm Valley is anything but fancy and multitudes of short-term renters may not be to your liking, but what you get for your money is impressive, as is the club's outstanding fiscal management.

Rancho Mirage Golf and Country Club

38-500 Bob Hope
Rancho Mirage, CA 92270
(760) 324-4711
http://www.ranchomiragegolf.com

Rancho Mirage Country Club is now a shell of its former self. Inaugurated in 1984 with 266 homes ranging from 1,700 to 3,200 square feet, until the middle of 2015, couples paid $5.4K for a golf membership and singles $3.9K. For this you got unlimited golf and

range balls. Residents HOAs averaged $490 monthly. Home prices started around $300K and reached $500K. That was then. The future now holds little for homeowners. Why? They never owned their golf course or clubhouse. A developer did. The owners defaulted to this developer and now belong to a homeowner association with homes but no golf course. The developer plans to build a retirement where the course once was. Predictably, home values have precipitously dropped. Enjoy the photos of this now-dead club. Next year's edition of this book will no longer include Rancho Mirage Golf and Country Club. May it rest in peace.

Shadow Mountain Resort

45750 San Luis Rey Avenue
Palm Desert, CA 92260
(760) 346-6123

This development/resort sports one of the Coachella Valley's finest tennis facilities. Shadow Mountain first opened in the late 1940's. Its 600 Condos include 400 square-foot studios along with 2,000 square foot three-bedroom condos. Asking prices range from $100K to $400K. The HOA runs between $300 and $500 per month, depending on whether the rate includes utilities, which most studio condos do. There's a heavy condo rental business brokered by the resort, meaning especially on winter weekends you'll find lots of non-members on the grounds. There's a tiny almost insignificant exercise room at the back of the pro shop, a basketball court and 16 lighted tennis courts to include clay, grass and hard court. The Resort's huge pool is reportedly the largest in the Coachella Valley.

This club is one of the few that can offer 4.5-USTA-rated-and-higher players enough fellow players for singles and doubles competition. Golf can be had at the adjacent and unaffiliated Shadow Mountain Golf Course. It's flat and not challenging but at least it's nearby. Shadow Mountain Resort condos don't remain long on the market. This gated community (in Winter) is within walking distance of El Paseo and down town Palm Desert. The

permanent resident community is tight, dinners are held during season in the restaurant on the second floor above the tennis pro shop.Two years ago, management changed hands. The state of the development's finances is unknown and not likely to be robust. That said, this is one of few gated communities that despite its age and rental traffic continues to attract new, younger members.

The Springs

One Duke Drive
Rancho Mirage, CA 92270
(760) 324-8292
http://springsclub.com

The Springs was established in 1975 on 385 acres across the street from the Eisenhower Medical Center. Its 46 community pools and 817 homes look well maintained but 'tired.' If you're a prospective resident, you can waive the $7.5K golf initiation fee for a year and pay golf dues of only $895 per month during that time. A full golf/tennis/etc. family membership costs $7.5K initiation plus $1,330 monthly dues, which includes a Social membership and tennis. Children, their spouses and grandchildren are included in this fee. If you only wish to play tennis, you pay $165 monthly with no

initiation fee. Home asking prices range from the high $300Ks to $800K. The monthly HOA has gone up a worrisome $111 in the past year and is now $915. Despite an escalating HOA, the Springs offers its residents a centrally located, pleasant place to live.

Silver Sands Racquet Club
74155 Country Club Drive
Palm Desert, CA 92260
(760) 340-1667
http://silversandshoa.com

This gated community sits adjacent to the J.W. Marriott Desert Springs Resort and across the street from the Desert Willow Golf Resort, where Silver Sands members can play for $48 a round. If a resident doesn't feel like golf or tennis, he or she can relax in any of the community's 15 pools. The complex was established in 1992. Condos are sized from 1,000 up to 1,900 SF. There are 15 tennis courts, eight of them lighted, and a tennis pro on staff in season. Home prices range from $200,000 to $450K.The HOAs run $556 per month, the same as last year. The club's Winter 2014 Newsletter reported that residents have approved the construction of an exercise room on space occupied by an unused racquetball court, suggesting younger members were requesting what older members didn't miss. A good sign. Another good sign: the community's website lists resident committees for monitoring landscaping, security, finance and maintenance. The Club seems to be well liked by residents, who in newsletter photos look prosperous, active and compatible. Realtor site activity suggests that units sell quickly.

The development's flat roofs are slowly being repaired/replaced but nothing was said about a one-time assessment to get this done, suggesting the club has ample reserves. If Silver Sands interests you, make sure to check its finances and whether there are special assessments pending.

Sunrise Country Club

71-601 Country Club Drive
Rancho Mirage, CA 92270
(760) 328-6549

This community's website opens with a series of panorama shots of the club, which looks beautiful lit up with a lake in front. Then there's the pool, which doesn't look all that inviting, a large lake with spouting underwater fountains that does, and a dining room that looks like a Denny's. This condominium community dates back to 1974 and was one of the first done by Bill Bone, who's

spurred much of the Coachella Valley's resort community development in the past 25 years. Sunrise has 746 homes, an executive par-64 18-hole golf course, driving range, practice greens, PGA-certified instructors, a pro shop, 12 tennis courts, three pickle ball courts, 21 swimming pools and 20 Jacuzzis. There's no golf initiation fee. Yearly course fees run $3,801 for a couple and $2,985 for an individual. Home prices range from $125K to the mid $300K's, with square footage from 854 to 2,127 square feet. The HOA varies from $444 to $550 monthly. There's a second monthly HOA of $235, which is paid to the club and functions as a Social membership fee. A lot of the units reportedly can use updating. I'd be leery about the average age of residents here. On the plus side, I don't see a lot of rental activity, which is good.

Woodhaven Country Club

41-555 Woodhaven Drive East

Palm Desert, CA 92211

(760) 345-7636

Opened in 1985, one local realtor touts Woodhaven and its 900 condos as one of the Coachella Valley's most affordable golf club communities. My overall impression is that it's an average sort of place. The golf course isn't challenging and there's nothing about the clubhouse, amenities or homes that stands out. The community's residents purchased the golf course, clubhouse and associated amenities (tennis courts, walking trails, etc.) in 2011. The golf course is open to the public. There's no golf initiation fee. A single membership costs $900 per month and a couples membership $1,200 monthly. If you pay for four months at one time, you get a 10% fee reduction. HOA dues run $495 monthly, up $74 a month from 2015. You can buy a six-month golf membership tailored to Canadians and other snowbirds. That's a good deal. Recent asking prices range from the low $200Ks to the mid $300Ks and range from 1,342 to 2,178 square feet. For fun, I read Yelp comments on the community. Most weren't favorable. The majority of complaints seemed petty but others reflected a lack of staff training. Tripadvisor.com reports from renters staying for a week or less were uniformly more favorable.

Summary

What characterizes mid-priced communities for me is their age, the predominance of condos, pools scattered hither and yon, and growing rental traffic.

Another signature difference: High-end communities demand and get upwards of $300K golf initiation fees. Upper Middle complexes want from $10K to $50K; but most mid-priced communities want $7,500 or less.*

Golf initiation costs are not all that differentiate the mid-priced residential resorts from the Upper-middle, although they are certainly influential to any buying decision.

Upper-middle communities convey a sense of privilege with their uniformed, solicitous staffs, spa massage services, concierges to do errands, and, of course a richer clientele.

The Valley's mid-priced communities, Bermuda Dunes, The Lakes and The Springs excepted, convey more of an egalitarian vibe. Their 'inclusiveness' resembles 55+ communities. Their house prices do as well. No one joins Woodhaven or Oasis for its prestige. People join because they're comfortable there.

Avondale, The Springs and Silver Sands strike me as best bets in the Mid-price group. I say this despite considerable respect for The Lakes and Shadow Mountain Resort.

I like The Springs because of its amenities and bigger homes, although the precipitous rise in HOA and monthly golf dues suggest budget problems.

Despite being part of the Coachella Valley tennis community and subbing at a variety of venues, I knew nothing about Silver Sands Racquet Club.

This community hasn't raised its HOA in two years —an excellent sign that its finances are in order.

Avondale also creates the impression that it is well run and works hard to serve its residents, to include children. The focus on children is almost unique in the Valley, Big Horn excepted.

Many mid-priced communities advertise their rental units on Tripadvisor.com and other travel sites, which suggest such developments have reached a tipping point with too many absentee owners not attending board meetings to protect their investment or assuring that needed work gets done.

Again, when buying a desert-gated community home, you have to ask yourself what's most important to you and how much you're willing to pay to get it.

You can play a round of golf at Sunrise and have just as much fun as a round at the Madison Club or Indian Ridge, but do both and you'd notice the difference.

Chart: Mid-priced Communities

Community	Golf Dues / Homes	Price	Debut	HOA	Monthly Fee	Golf
Avondale	$700K	1969	$750	$3K	$850	305
Bermuda Dunes	$700K	1959	$300	$2.5K	$848	200
Chaparral	$275K	1979	$420	$5.5K	$110	625
Desert Falls	$350K	1988	$435	$N/A	$N/A	900
Indian Palms	$250K	1974	$225	None	None	3,000
Indian Springs	$350K	1962	$266	$5K	None	709
The Lakes	$275K	1985	$1,100	$10K	$545	902
Monterrey	$300K	1979	$474	$7K	$435	1,206
Oasis	$275K	1983	$520	$3K	None	662
Mar'kesh	$250K	1967	$905	$15K	$200	364
Palm Desert Tennis	$225K	1973	$515	None	None	100
Palm Valley	$400K	1983	$574	$3.5K	$430	1,274
Rancho Mirage	$325K	1984	$490	Course closed	Course closed	266
Shadow Mountain	$250K	1966	$395	None	None	100
The Springs	$500K	1975	$790	$7.5K	$895	817
Silver Sands	$350K	1981	$556	None	None	250
Sunrise	$230K	1974	$763	$3.4K	None	746
Wood'avn	$250K	1984	$421	$6K	None	940

Mid-price communities
Estimated monthly expense

Community	HOA/golf	Est. Utilities	Est. * Prop.Tax*	Total
The Springs	$2,243	$300	$325	$2,868
Avondale	$1,550	$300	$325	$2,175
The Lakes	$1,645	$300	$325	$2,125
Bermuda Dunes	$1,148	$300	$650	$2,098
Marrakesh	$1,105	$300	$325	$1,730

Average: $1,563

Community	HOA/golf	Est. Utilities	Est. * Prop.Tax*	Total
Palm Valley	$1,004	$300	$325	$1,629
Rancho Mirage	$990	300	$325	$1,615
Monterrey	$909	$300	$325	$1,534
Woodhaven	$888	$300	$325	$1,513
Sunrise	$763	$300	$325	$1.328
Desert Falls	$435	$300	$325	$1,160
Chaparral	$530	$300	$325	$1,155
Silver Sands	$556	$300	$300	$1,116
Indian Springs	$266	$300	$325	$1,081
Shadow Mountain	$400	$300	$300	$1,000
Indian Palms	$225	$300	$325	$850

Notes

At 1.2% of home assessed at $300,000, equaling property tax of $300 per month.

Shadow Mountain and Silver Sands do not have golf courses, so they have no golf initiation fee or monthly golf dues.

It's recommended that you do your own costing based on this model, plugging in your own numbers to see where you fit on the continuum shown above.

In addition to the prices you've just noted, your utilities (Gas/Electricity/Internet/Cable TV/Water) will average another $300-$400 per month on average.

Telephone, Internet and cable TV service may be purchased seasonally (November through May). Check   to make sure. Costs vary by city and community, so   check to make sure.

Maid service for a 2,000-square-foot house runs $75-$100 every two weeks, or $150-$200 per month. Double that $ amount for a 4,000-square-foot house.

A gardener will charge $85-$100 per month for a 2,000-square-foot house and double that $ amount for a 4,000-square foot house, depending, of course, on the   size of the lot.

If you have a pool, its maintenance will set you back another $100 per month.

Thus, owning a Mid-priced house in a Coachella Valley gated community, could hypothetically cost:

Average monthly HOA/Golf/ Utilities/Property Tax:	$1,561
Maid service twice monthly	$150
Gardener monthly	$85
Monthly pool maintenance	$100
Total:	$1,896

Conclusion: **Budget $2,200 monthly** to operate your mid-priced home in the desert.

Bargain Communities

Bargain Communities
Homes costing $50K to $150K

NOTE: *Statistics are taken from the public domain, realtor and gated community websites and brochures. These websites aren't always updated, meaning the data may be old and possibly wrong. The author has made every effort to include the latest and most accurate data. If you spot an error, let us know at jbarnes3609@gmail.com*

Bargain gated community homes range from 1,000 to 2,000 square feet and cost from $50K to $240K. A single contractor builds the tract houses, or, in the case of a 'manufactured' home or RV, the house is trucked to the site and hooked up to existing utilities.

Homes will be close together, and most will have two bedrooms and a den, although double-wides' may have three bedrooms. In manufactured home communities, almost no one will have a private yard and the garage will likely be a carport, although many homes will face the golf course or have a golf-course view.

HOA dues will tend under $300 monthly and amenities will mimic those of 55+ or Mid-price communities, have their own board of directors, invite guest speakers and encourage socialization. Communities without 'manufactured' housing will be old and cater mostly to renters.

Cathedral Canyon Country Club

68311 Paseo Real
Cathedral City, CA 92234
(760) 328-6571

Open in 1975 on land once owned by bandleader Lawrence Welk, an annual Cathedral Canyon golf single membership here costs $2,499 and a family one $3,499, although you can golf for $25 on some days, to include the cart. Condo units run 1,029 to almost 3,000 square feet and are located in multiple-unit, two-story buildings that face a 18-hole golf course dotted with 16 lakes. The lowest price I've seen is $85K and the highest $321K for a 2,700 square foot unit, but the average condo here can be had for $100K to $150K. There are 18 different HOAs with monthly dues averaging $400 to

$450. Each resident also pays a $1,461 land-lease fee. A few four-bedroom homes built in 1985 range upwards of 3,351-square-feet priced in the $400K's with a $750 monthly HOA. Cathedral Canyon's golf course is comprised of three nine-hole courses

he Cathedral Canyon clubhouse.

played in three different 18-hole combinations. Yelp reports problems with golf carts stalling, people walking their dogs on the course, crabby marshals and long lines at the tees. Most homes appear to be daily and longer rentals.

Deep Canyon Tennis Club

73120 Frank Feltrop Drive
Palm Desert, CA 92260
(760) 568-6822

This 70-acre development was built from 1974 to 1979 and contains 667 two- and three-bedroom condos, either on ground level or on the second floor. Each of the complex's 350 2- and 3-bedroom condos has its own carport. You'll find 12 tennis courts, six pickle ball   courts, two tennis pros, 24 swimming pools, a putting green, work-out room, library and a clubhouse focused around tennis. Condos range from 1,088 to 1,258 square feet and cost from the high $180's to $250K. The HOA monthly fee runs $514. The club boasts of more PTA-certified 4.0 and 4.5 players than anywhere else in the Coachella Valley other than Shadow Mountain Resort. It fields competitive teams in all the leagues and at all levels. I've participated in league play here, liked the place and enjoyed the   people but had no idea the homes were so small. Resale prices seem to be holding steady, but I'd check the average age of members before committing.

Desert Princess Country Club

28822 Desert Princess Drive
Cathedral City, CA 922234
(760) 322-1907 ext. 102

Realtors will tell you this is one of the Valley's most affordable country clubs. That conclusion references Desert Princess' relatively low home prices likely caused by higher-than-average HOA dues, which we'll get to in a moment. So what are the actual costs? An annual golf membership for an individual resident runs $3.5K and for a couple $5.9K. Real estate includes 675 condos and 408 individual homes ranging from 800 to 2,400 square feet. Prices range from $69.5K to $340K, with a median price of $197K per one realtor group's estimate. In development from 1995 to 2005, all units face

a public golf course featuring 27 holes, 21 lakes and 85 sand traps. Members can enjoy 32 community pools, nine tennis courts, one basketball and two pickle ball courts, a hot tub, sauna, spa and menu of spa services, bocce ball, a restaurant open all day and into

the evening, and horseshoes; but remember: these facilities must be shared with flocks of day visitors plus overnight and weekend renters. The HOA runs $580 monthly, and on top of that there's a land-lease fee that adds an additional $85 to $125. Rental units are listed on a variety of sites. expedia.com rated Desert Princess 3.5 on a scale of 1-5. Not a ringing endorsement.

Indian Palms Country Club

48630 Monroe Street
Indio, CA 92201
(760) 347-2326

When I first got to the Desert, a realtor drove me into this gated

d community. Six minutes moving down badly maintained streets, I saw small houses, many not well maintained, plus old cars and trucks parked in driveways. I told the realtor to turn around and leave. You may get a more favorable impression. Improvements may have been made. It's over six years since I've set foot in there.

The 643-acre development opened in 1948. Its golf course was completely redone in 2003.It has two pools, a fitness center and five tennis courts. There are 18 separate HOAs. ranging from $4140 to $478 per month with the average running around $250. Most of the   homes were built from 1978 on. Home/condo asking prices range from $90K, 616-square-foot studios to $478K, 2,300 to 2,900 square golf course homes. Indian Palms has approximately 3000 residences and many different contractors have built houses here, so you won't find a uniform home style.

A 59-room hotel, the Indian Palms sits inside the gates along with a restaurant. Pictures on its website make the hotel look   like a two-story motel from the 1950s. Craig's List has rentals in Indian Palms for $850 per month.

Mesquite Country Club

2700 Mesquite Avenue
Palm Springs, CA 92264
(760) 323-9377
www.golfnow.com/mesquite

Opened over 30 years ago, Mesquite looks it. The web site show beautiful vistas but photos on Yelp show sand traps on this club's golf course badly in need of weeding. Also, there must be a lot of rentals here. You can find them on Tripadvisor.com, espedia.com, booking.com, vrbo.com and similar sites. As far as I know, Mesquite is the only gated resort community in Palm Springs. Mesquite's clubhouse is 'classic' Spanish style and has an elevated restaurant and banquet hall overlooking the golf course and mountains. Last year, non-residents or residents could pay $2.6K for a single and $3.6K for a family, and $2.1K if over age 55. This year, I'm told, no such annual 'memberships' are available.

Residents with proper I.D. do get a discount on golf carts. In 2010, the city of Palm Springs took over the course. Mesquite Country Club itself was closed temporarily in 2013. Palm Springs poured $2M into the property to whip it back in shape. Six hundred condominiums remain. Their recent prices (February 2016) run

from $149K for a 707 one-bedroom to as high as $267K for a 1,175 square-foot, two-bedroom condo. Realtor websites show houses on the market for as much as a year without a sale. Residents regardless of size of unit pay HOA dues of $420 monthly. These condos are distributed within 33 acres mixed with Spanish fountains, 16 swimming pools and 18 hot tubs. Mesquite offers renters, vacationers and residents eight tennis and two racquetball courts, bike paths and a golf course with five lakes, seven bridges and 800 palm trees. Residents must be thanking the gods for Palm Springs' intervention and for the play of outsiders. Otherwise they'd be without a club.

Outdoor Resort Palm Springs

69-411 Ramon Road
Cathedral City, CA 92234
760-328-3834

If you own a motor home and live within three days drive of Palm Springs, California, you should give consideration to this nearby (Cathedral City) Outdoor Resort. It offers 1,218 individually

owned fee simple lots, each with 50-amp electrical services, water, two phone connections and cable TV. Lots run from $49K to $160K depending on their closeness to one of two clubhouses and whether pavers   and other enhancements have been added. Some owners will even toss add their already-hooked up and operational RV into the deal.Rentals run from $700 to $1,600 per month in season (November to May). Summer rates drop to $50 per night and $500 per week, although why anyone would want to live in a mobile home in 115-degree heat remains a mystery, although an owner here said that about 50 couples do indeed stay all year long.

Outdoor Resort's 137 enclosed acres come with 24- hour gated and patrolled security, seven lakes, a 27- hole, par-three golf course, 14 lighted tennis courts, eight pools, ten spas, a café, hair salon, barber shop, expresso bar, fitness center, billiard and card rooms, lounge, laundry, theater and convenience store. The usual line-dancing, card games, tennis, golf, sit-down dinners and other activities are offered and the monthly HOA dues are low $325 per month. I played in a tennis tournament here in February and afterwards talked with members who uniformly praised Outdoor Resorts, which is self-managed with its own board of directors. Members come from as far north as Vancouver with a heavy contingent from the Seattle, Portland, Oregon, northern California and Orange county. Best of all, downtown Palm Springs is but a ten=minute drive.

Palm Desert Resort

77333 Country Club Drive
Palm Desert, CA 92211
(760) 345-2781

Opened in 1980, Palm Desert Resort has 960 flat-roofed condo homes measuring 938 to 1,400 square feet, each with an attached two-car garage. A golf membership   costs $3.5K with $390 monthly dues. These relatively small condos fall in the $150K to $250K range. The HOA runs $405 monthly plus $42 monthly to the golf course for a total of $447 monthly. In addition, each

residential property is expected to spend a minimum of $400 annually in the restaurant.

Residents have use of 14 tennis courts with a stadium court seating 1,500. Tennis membership will cost a couple $125 per month. I've played here. The tennis facilities equal those of any Upper-middle club. That said, you get the sense this place is struggling. Both the buildings and the residents appear on the old side,   although a robust sense of community resonates. One final caveat: There are a lot of rentals here, suggesting much itinerant traffic. I'd be wary, although for the price Palm Desert remains an attractive proposition.

Portola Country Club

42-500 Portola Avenue
Palm Desert, CA 93360
760-346-5481

This manufactured home community was opened in1974 before double-pane windows, granite counter tops, pickle ball and other changes in amenities became   popular in desert communities.This is not to say this community doesn't have a lot to offer —it does. The HOA for such an ancient place is still only $298 and home prices range from $95K to $269K, meaning they are available to a lot   of retirees without a lot of money. Golf is free for residents, there's a clubhouse, workout room, banquet facilities plus pick-up card games and paths for walking. Homes number 500 and range from 1,152 to1,920 square feet and include a two-car carport. The club is close to Palm desert's El Paseo's shops and restaurants plus the Westgate and other shopping centers. What remains problematic is the age of this community and the number of rentals. I've seen nightly rents of $55 per night offered on some vacation sites. What Portola Country Club has going for it is its proximity to Palm Desert's

attractions and the low cost. For some, this will be more than enough.

Summary

You get what you pay for, right? Not necessarily. Begin with the bare bones of any resort. There's a golf course or golf courses, a clubhouse, homes, tennis and bocce ball courts, a pool or pools, and a restaurant. Throw a wall around this community and now it's gated. Add a resident board of directors, hire a management company and maintenance workers to keep order, and you're in business.

Almost every community we've discussed in this book offers these bare bones, to include the bargain communities we've just examined. Now we start forming comparisons. How old is the community? Age makes a difference. Here's why.

Each new generation demands changes. For example, residents retiring to the desert in 2010 and later want fully equipped gyms and aren't interested in the racquet ball courts built in the 1990s. Now pickle ball is the preferred new sport.

Condo communities are out of favor. They have proven not to work as well as freestanding homes because condo owners are on the hook for repairs (roofs, repainting, etc.) on not just their unit but those of their neighbors as well.

If a condo community doesn't have sufficient reserves, and most don't, special $ assessments are levied on residents that can exceed $20K.

Scattering pools everywhere no longer makes sense either. A friend a PGA West who recently left said there were pools everywhere in his development and nobody used them. Larger single pools get used when they offer a chance to socialize and be seen.

The flat roofs of older developments also don't work as well as pitched roofs, or is that just a change in buyers' preferences? I don't know, but I do notice a lot of flat roofs in older communities and none in the newer ones. Ergo, flat roofs become associated with what's 'outdated.'

Another age tip-off, lack of stainless steel kitchen appliances and marble, granite and other stone finishes not only in kitchens but in bathrooms. Twenty years ago this was not expected. Today it is.

None of this carping affects those who choose bargain-priced communities. People choose such communities because they're cheap, the amenities they want are they and don't have to pay an arm and a leg to enjoy them.

It's a shame that new bargain-priced developments aren't being built. I suspect the economics of land acquisition, development and marketing militate against building new communities at this low a price point.

For that matter, one can argue that the only workable resorts are the 55+ ones because they have large numbers of residents, aren't condo-centric and have the resident $$ to support golf courses and other amenities. Then there are the high-end gated communities. They'll survive as well. Members will happily pay whatever it costs to maintain them.

What does this presage for Upper-middle and mid-priced gated communities in the southern California desert? Trouble the long term, unless young people suddenly take to golf.

Comparison Chart
Bargain Communities

Community	City	Price	Debut	Monthly HOA	Golf Fee	Golf Dues	Homes
Cathedral Canyon	Cathedral City	$125K	1975	$465	None	$395	300
Deep Canyon	Palm Desert	$200K	1974	$514	None	None	350
Desert Princess	Cathedral City	$225K	1985	$56	None	$85	1,083
Mesquite	Palm Desert	$225K	1985	$200	$200	$270	600
Palm Desert Resort	Palm Desert	$200K	1980	$43	$3.5K	$430	960

Bargain Communities
Ownership Costs

Community	HOA/golf	Utilities	est. Prop/tax	est. Total
Palm Desert Resort	$869	$300	$200	$1,369
Cathedral Canyon	$860	$300	$125	$1,285

Average $1,066 monthly

Deep Canyon	$514	$300	$200	$1,014
Mesquite	$470	$300	$225	$995
Desert Princess	$141	$300	$225	$666

Notes

Be aware. These $ amounts show fixed on-going monthly expenses <u>even if you're not there</u>. It's recommended that you do your own costing based on this model, plugging in your own numbers to see where you fit on the continuum shown above.

Your property tax, if you carry a mortgage, maybe included in your monthly mortgage payment. If so, extract and add it. Utilities (Gas/ Electricity/Internet/Cable TV/Water) will average another $250-$325 per month on average.

Telephone, Internet and cable TV service may be purchased seasonally (November through May), but check to make sure as this may vary from city to   city.

<u>Maid service for a home of 2,000 square feet or less runs $75</u> every two weeks, or $150 per month.

<u>A gardener will charge $85-$100 per month</u> for a 2,000-square-foot house.

<u>If you have a pool, its maintenance will set you back another $100 per month.</u>

Thus, monthly expenses associated with owning a non-mortgaged, bargain-priced gated-community home in a Coachella Valley could hypothetically cost:

HOA/golf/utilities/property tax.......$1,006 monthly
      Housekeeper...................... $175
      Gardener.......................... $85
      Pool................................ $100
           Grand total: **$1366**

Conclusion: Budget **$1,400 monthly** to operate your bargain gated-community home.

Summary and what you must decide before you buy

If you've read this far, you now know more about desert gated communities in both a macro and micro sense than most Desert realtors.

I found it surprising the choices one has with $1M+ to spend on a desert vacation house; but financing the house is only a portion of the total transaction.

Go 'High End' and you also pay upwards of $350K for a golf/social membership. Some gated communities will demand the money at the time you sign the housing contract.

Buy a $1M+ place in an Upper Middle range and the golf/membership costs won't exceed $75K.

Buy in a mid-price community at that membership cost drops to $10 to $12K and less.

To review: Total loosely estimated average monthly operating costs monthly HOA fee, golf fee, utility costs (telephone, Internet, gas, electricity, water), housekeeper and pool maintenance added, are as follows:

High-end.......................$6,000
Upper-middle.................. $4,000
Mid-priced.................... $2,200
Bargain..................... $1,400
55+........................... $1,400

How to change these numbers: For those of you not interested in High-end or Upper-middle communities, you can reduce your monthly expenses by having a maid only once a month or not at all.

You can buy a home with no pool and use the pool(s) your community provides.

If you only use your home five months a year, you can shut off some utilities when you're not there.

Why do 55+ communities have the lowest operational costs? They don't charge a monthly fee (Trilogy La Quinta and Heritage Palms being exceptions) for using the golf course.

That makes them three times cheaper than a high-end gated community and 2.5 times less expensive than an Upper-middle community.

55+ communities also don't charge a golf initiation fee, which as you've read, can be 250K at some clubs and required up front at the time you buy.

Why doesn't everyone opt for the 55+ community? One obvious reason: you have to be 55 years old to buy a home there.

Also, 55+ home prices trend $100K to $300K more expensive on average than bargain-priced communities, making bargain-priced developments more attractive to the budget conscious.

Okay, but why choose a mid-priced community over a 55+ community?

The only reason I justify is that you want to buy in the desert but you won't be 55 for a while.

Why choose an upper-middle community over a55+ community? Here the answer is clear.

Prestige. No one's impressed if you tell them you livein a 55+ community. Plus you get free cookies in the lobby, an on-hand handyman to fix leaky faucets, a concierge to buy your groceries and get you theater tickets and restaurant reservations.

The golf course and tennis courts will be supported by pro shops and resident pros. You'll enjoy bars and lounges and reasonably good food. 55+communities offer none of this.

Okay, so why choose a high-end community over an Upper-middle one?

An upper-middle place name may impress. A high-end name can provoke awed silence. Plus, you'll be with people rich enough to guarantee your shared surroundings stay pristine, up to date and provide you with privacy and the chance to mingle with select others like yourself.

Suggestion: If you have $1M+ to spend on a house, who says it needs to be in a high-end, upper-middle or mid-priced community?

You can buy a $1M+ house in a Rancho Mirage, Palm Desert or La Quinta gated subdivision, pay $500 monthly or less for HOA dues and enjoy golf at any of the semi-public golf courses attached to semi-public, upper-middle and mid-priced communities and save a ton of money.

Let's say your budget's $500K.

If you're patient, you can sometimes find in a condo inside a high-end community for $500K, but again, you'll still need over $200K for a Golf/Social membership and will have $4K monthly operational expenses, so maybe that's not the solution.

If you spend $500K to live in a 55+ community,you'll actually get more 'goodies' than even in high-end communities, to include two golf courses, ndoor and outdoor pools, community-sponsored comedy clubs, pottery rooms and the like; but you'll do without the pro shop, the attendants dressed like   Swiss Army cadets and the prestige and sense of success you'll get associating with the nation's business and government leaders.

Country Club versus no Country Club

Recently I met a friend for breakfast in Palm Desert. He once lived in The Springs but now lives in Sun City Palm Desert, a 55+ community. I asked what differences he noted.

At the Springs there was a bar next to the men's golf locker room," he said, "plus a lounge. If my wife called, the bartender would say I wasn't there. That's an example of personal service. We have more   facilities here at Sun City, and some, like the gym, are superior, but we lack the personal service and a good restaurant, and that can make a difference."

So how should you use this knowledge?

Let's start with the city you choose to live in. You'll impress some people with an Indian Wells address. If you're choosing between two 'equal' communities and one's in Indian Wells, location might be enough to break the tie.

But be careful. Regardless of the city, you don't want to be near a trash dump, power plant or even open land and the dust it generates. So check on what's outside the gates of every community that interests you.

If there's desert on the other side of the wall, you're likely to get sand storms. I have a friend at The Lakes who said that people north of 'The Ten' get more sand in their homes than those living south of the Ten. I have no idea if this is true.

Also, what if there's tilled, crop-growing land outside the gates, or a noisy road? Or a dog park next door? Or a noisy freeway or train track? You should consider all of this before buying.

Also, do you want your house to face south. Many long-time Desert residents say this is best because you get the morning sun but it never shines in.

Golf? Social membership?

Almost all gated communities offer golf, and for those who don't play there are Social memberships.

At the high end in particular, you may not have a choice. You have to pay for the golf. Most lower-priced communities let you pick between Golf and Social, or choose both.

Some clubs will give you a discount if you buy both. Some clubs include the Social with a golf membership. Some clubs separate tennis and pickle ball from a Social, meaning you buy all, some or choose among Golf, Social and Sports memberships.

How do such costs compare with the competition? Check the Comparison Charts at the end of each section and the back of this book.

Compare quality.

Once you decide how you'll be spending time in your gated community, consider the overall quality of the facilities. Does staff keep the floors, grass and other surfaces clean?

Older developments offer a spare room with exercise equipment. Newer developments have gorgeous exercise facilities that have an unimpeded view of the golf course, fountains and the like.

If you play golf, consider the course. You're going to be playing it a lot. Is it flat and uninteresting? Do you care?

Will amenities be there when you are?

Will you live full time in the desert? If so, make sure the facilities in your community you use are available year-around.

What's happening to home prices?

Use Zillow.com to check addresses of homes you might wish to buy. Zillow will show what the last two or three owners paid. Do this with neighboring houses as well. Are prices headed up or down? If the trend's downward, you've been warned.

The biggest mistake I've found that when moving from a big city to a desert community, buyers fall in love with a house without considering total quality of life both inside   and outside their community.

Don't let a realtor steer you to one or two developments he or she is most familiar with or   where there are homes or resales represented by her real estate company.

Do your homework. Your realtor can do a better job helping you find the right community if you already   know what you don't want. Then tell your realtor what you do want. This book will give you the overview and structure you need to help your realtor serve you better.

How close are you to what you need?

Before you buy, drive from your chosen community to buy a quart of milk, a bottle of gin, food, get a car repaired, eat at a good restaurant, get a haircut or have your shoes resoled. How long did it take?

Imagine if for even the most mundane need you have to drive more than 20 minutes each way. Imagine doing that twice a day two or three times a week.

Are there enough of the 'right' people for you?

If you've fallen in love with a smaller community(Under 1,000 homes), consider whether there's a sufficient nucleus to populate the activities you like.

For example, almost all clubs offer tennis, but few have enough players at the 3.0, 3.5 and 4.0 levels to guarantee matches, meaning you may have to drive somewhere else to find decent competition.

Golf course lot or privacy lot?

In most communities you can pay upwards of $100K extra to face a golf course. You may only get half of that back when you sell.

In some developments everybody across the fairway may be able to see when you get up, leave the house and go to bed; plus you may have to carry extra insurance when golf balls break windows or roof tiles.

Privacy lots don't have people across the fairway looking in, but they often don't provide privacy either. In mid-price, 55+ and bargain-comfortable communities you may have houses on both sides of you and another facing you in your back yard.

Will you be blind-sided by special assessments?

By all means check out a community's $ reserves. In the past three years, have residents paid one-time assessments over and above the monthly HOA dues?   If so, how much? What's likely to be next? Read old Board reports. Often they'll tip you off.

Condo or freestanding home?

Condos will cost you less but in all-condo communities there will be constant maintenance that includes not only the grounds and facilities but the condos themselves. I've heard of new roofs costing each homeowner $40K in special assessments.

So buying a condo may save you money in the initial purchase but end up saddling you with unanticipated assessments later. Own your own freestanding home and you're responsible for its roof but nobody else's.

Technically, it's the community's and your realtor's obligation to inform you of upcoming assessments before you buy, but that doesn't always happen.

If you opt for a freestanding home, how old is it? If the home's over ten years old, when were the air-conditioner, furnace, plumbing, electrical, water heater, etc.last replaced?

Do you have children?

Is the community child- and grand child friendly? Will there be enough for them to do? How many   bedrooms will you need to house them?

Are your community's expenses due for a sudden rise?

Older communities require constant updating. Check out not only the cost of the monthly HOA but how much it's risen in the past five years.

Before you buy, ask for Board amortization reports. Have your realtor or a CPA sit down with you and examine them.

These amortization reports will tell you when replacements are scheduled, what the community has budgeted for them and if the cost will be handled by reserves already collected for that purpose.

Ask when the HOA payment will have to be raised to keep reserves at the California state-required level   and how much the raise will be. You might get lucky and actually get your question answered.

If the community you're interested in is old (built from 1960-1990), be aware that golf course sprinkler systems, roofs, landscaping, addition of pickle ball courts, repaving and other repairs, if they've not been done, will have to be done, often sooner than later.

How does everybody get along?

One community I've mentioned had fistfights in a Board meeting accompanied, supposedly, by gay slurs.Not the best advertisement for a happy community. Check around, so check in with me from time to time. It can't hurt.

What are the rules?

The HOA must publish any that apply to all residents. Do they seem overly draconian? Ask residents. Some 55+ communities will charge you $200 if while inside the community you or your vendor fails to stop at a stop sign or are speeding.

After using the tables provided to chart your likely expenses, consider these added possibilities:

Many High-end and Upper-middle ranked communities require you to spend X amount of $ for meals in the clubhouse dining room. If so, how much?

There may be greens fees and cart fees. If so, what are they?

Is tipping not permitted? If so, are there exceptions, or, are you expected to kick $1,000 or some other amount into a general pot at Christmas time to reward and incentivize the help?

Does X gated community looked 'dated' to you? If so, consider looking elsewhere.

Is governance done by residents or outside company? Do you care?

Finally, if for any reason you feel uncomfortable about a place that interests you, take time to identify what's bothering you and talk it over with your spouse and your realtor. Don't buy unless you're absolutely sure you've answered all the above questions to your satisfaction.

So that's it. Your due diligence is done.

You like where your gated community's situated.

You've decided between Golf and Social memberships.

You've chosen a privacy or golf-course-facing lot.

There are no special assessments on the horizon.

House prices in the community are stable or rising.

The HOA hasn't been rising precipitously.

Residents seem to get along.

You don't feel like you're in a concentration camp.

The quality of your surroundings is high.

There are enough people for activities you and your family like.

You're close to supermarkets and other stuff.

You sign the requisite papers and make your move.

Was it worth it? Has this book neglected anything important?

Let me know. Write down your experiences and email them to my website   jbarnes3609@gmail.com

Thanks, and here's hoping you experience many wonderful years of Desert living.

John J. Barnes
jbarnes3609@gmail.com

Alphabetical Listing

of Gated Communities

Andalusia at Coral Mountain, Page 60
Avenue 58 at Madison
La Quinta, CA 922
(760) 777-1000
andalusiaatcoralmountain.com

Avondale Country Club , Page 196
75-300 Avondale Drive
Palm Desert, CA
(760) 345-2727
avondalegolfclub.com

Bajada Estates, Page 105
Dry Creek Road south of Avenue 50
La Quinta, CA 92253

Bermuda Dunes Country Club, Page 198
42360 Adams Street
Bermuda Dunes, CA 9220
(760) 345-2771
www.bermudadunescc.org

Big Horn, Page 62
255 Palowet Drive
Palm Desert, Ca 92260
(760) 341-4653

Cathedral Canyon Country Club, Page 243
68311 Paseo Real
Cathedral City, CA 92234
(760) 328-6571

Chaparral Country Club, Page 201
100 Chaparral Drive
Palm Desert CA 92260
(760) 340-1893

The Citrus Club, Page 106
50-503 Mandarina
La Quinta, Ca 92253
(760) 564-7620

Deep Canyon Tennis Club, Page 245
73120 Frank Feltrop Drive
Palm Desert, CA 92260
(760) 568-6822

Desert Falls Country Club, Page 203
1111 Desert Falls Parkway
Palm Desert, CA 92211
(760) 340-5646

Desert Horizons(H), Page 95
44900 Desert Horizons Drive
Indian Wells, CA 92210
(760) 340-1871
www.deserthorizonscc.com

Desert Princess Country Club, Page 247
28822 Desert Princess Drive
Cathedral City, CA 922234
(760) 322-1907 ext. 102

Duna La Quinta, Page 122
78255 Avenue 50
La Quinta, CA 92253
(760) 564-7592
www.laquintaresort.com

El Dorado Country Club, Page 64
46000 East Eldorado Drive
Indian Wells, CA 92210
(760) 346-8081

Enclave Estates, Page 107
Mountain Estates, Page 108
49-499 Eisenhower Drive
La Quinta, CA 92253
(760) 564-4111
www.laquintaresort.com

Fairway Estates, Page 132
34-600 Mission Hills Drive
Rancho Mirage, CA 92270
(760) 324-9400
missionhillssales.com

Haciendas at La Quinta Resort,Page 110
49-499 Eisenhower Drive
La Quinta, CA 92253
(760) 564-4111
www.laquintaresort.com

Heritage Palms, Page 106
44-291 South Heritage Palms Dr.
Indio, CA 92201
(760) 772-5755

Hidden Canyon, Page 123
77928 Desert Drive
La Quinta, CA 92253

Hovnanian Palm Springs, Page 168
1800 Sand Canyon
Palm Springs, CA 92262
(86)-347-7116 or (888)-287-2490

Hovnanian Terra Lago, Page 170
8400 Terra Lago Parkway
Indio, CA 92203
(888) 631-1006
www.khov4seasons.com/4-seasons-terra-lago

Hideaway, Page 68
80-440 Hideaway Club Court
La Quinta, CA 9225
(760) 777-7400

Indian Palms Country Club, Page 249
48630 Monroe Street
Indio, CA 92201
(760) 347-2326
www.indianpalms.com

Indian Ridge, Page 97
76375 Country Club Drive
Palm Desert, CA 92211
(760) 772-7272
www.indianridgecc.com

Indian Springs, Page 205
79940 Westward Ho Drive
Indio, CA 9220
(760) 200-8988
http://www.indianspringsgc.com

Indian Wells Country Club, Page 99
46000 East Eldorado Drive
Indian Wells, CA 92210
 (760) 345-2561

Ironwood Country Club, Page 101
73735 Irontree Drive
Palm Desert, CA
(760) 346-0551

Ivey Ranch Country Club, Page172
74580 Varner Road,
Thousand Palms, CA 92276
(760)-343-2013
iveyranchgolf.com

Lago La Quinta, Page 124
77-750 Avenue
La Quinta, Ca 92256
(760) 564=4151

Laguna La Paz, Page 125
Eisenhower near Avenue 50
La Quinta, CA 92253

Lakefront 1 and 11, Page 133
34-600 Mission Hills Drive
Rancho Mirage, CA 92270
(760) 324-9400
missionhillssales.com

The Lakes, Page 207
161 Old Ranch Road
Palm Desert, CA 92211
(760)568-4321

La Quinta Country Club, Page 119
77-750 Avenue 50
La Quinta, CA 92253
(760) 564=4151

La Quinta Fairways, Page 109
78995 Muirfield Way
La Quinta, CA 92253
(760) 564-1442
laquintafairways.com

La Quinta Resort and Club, Page 103
49-499 Eisenhower Drive
La Quinta, CA 92253
(760) 564-4111
www.laquintaresort.com

La Quinta Tennis Villas, Page 118
77-750 Avenue 50
La Quinta, CA 92253

(760) 564=4151
www.laquintatennisvillas.com

Legacy Oakhurst, Page 134
34-600 Mission Hills Drive
Rancho Mirage, CA 92270
(760) 324-9400
missionhillssales.com

Legacy Villas, Page 111
77-750 Avenue 50
La Quinta, CA 92253
(760) 564=4151

Los Estados, Page 112
13849-499 Eisenhower
La Quinta, CA 92253
(760) 564-4111
www.laquintaresort.com

Madison Club, Page 70
53035 Meriwether Way
La Quinta, Ca 92253
(760) 777-9320

Marrakesh Country Club, Page 211
47000 Marrakesh Drive,
Palm Desert, Ca 92260
 (760) 568-2268
www.marrakeshcountryclub.com

Mesquite Country Club, Page 251
2700 Mesquite Avenue
Palm Springs, CA 92264
(760) 323-9377

www.golfnow.com/mesquite

Mission Hills Country Club, Page 128
34-600 Mission Hills Drive
Rancho Mirage, CA 92270
(760) 324-9400
missionhillssales.com

Mission Hills East, Page 130
34-600 Mission Hills Drive
Rancho Mirage, CA 92270
(760) 324-9400
missionhillssales.com

Mission Haciendas, Page 136
34-600 Mission Hills Drive
Rancho Mirage, CA 92270
(760) 324-9400
missionhillssales.com

Mission Hills Tennis Villas, Page 131
34-600 Mission Hills Drive
Rancho Mirage, CA 92270
(760) 324-9400
missionhillssales.com

Monterey Country Club, Page 247
41-500 Monterey Avenue
Palm Desert, CA 92260
(760) 568-9311
www.montereycc.com

Monterro Estates,Page 153
Washington Street at Avenue 50

La Quinta, CA 92253

Morningside Country Club, Page 167
39033 Morningside Drive
Rancho Mirage, CA 92270
(760) 324-1234

Mountain View Country Club, Page 169
80-375 Pomelo
La Quinta, CA 92253
(760) 771-4311
www.mountainviewatlaquinta.com

Oasis Country Club, Page 249
43-300 Casbah Way
Palm Desert, CA 92260
(760) 200-0522
https://www.theoasiscountryclub.com

Outdoor Resort —Indio, Page 253
80-394 Avenue 48
Indio, A 92201
800-892-2992

Outdoor Resort —Palm Springs, Page 291
69-411 Ramon Road
Cathedral City, CA 92234
760-328-3834

Painted Cove, Page 139
Avenue 50 and Park Avenue
La Quinta, CA 92253

Pamilla, Page 140
Avenue 50 near Jefferson Street
La Quinta, CA 92253

Palms, Page 171
57000 Palms Drive
La Quinta, CA 92253
(760) 771-0297
www.thepalmsgc.org

Point Happy, Page 141
Washington Avenue south
of Highway 111
La Quinta, CA 92253

Palm Desert Greens, Page 205
26573-750 Country Club Drive
Palm Desert, CA 92260
(760) 346-2679
http://www.pdgcc.com

Palm Desert Resort, Page 293
77333 Country Club Drive
Palm Desert, CA 92211
(760) 345-2781

Palm Desert Tennis Club, Page 255
48240 Racquet Lane
Palm Desert, CA
(760) 346-5683
palmdeserttennisclub.com

Palm Valley Country Club, Page 257
76501 Begonia Lane
Palm Desert, CA 92211

(760) 345-2737

PGA West, Page 173
55-955 PGA Boulevard
La Quinta, CA 92255
(760) 564-7111
www.pgawest.com

PGA West Greg Norman Course, Page 175
55-955 PGA Boulevard
La Quinta, CA 92255
(760) 564-7111
www.pgawest.com

PGA West Legends Course, Page 175
55-955 PGA Boulevard
La Quinta, CA 92255
(760) 564-7111
www.pgawest.com

PGA West Tom Weiskopf Course, Page 175
55-955 PGA Boulevard
La Quinta, CA 92255
(760) 564-7111
www.pgawest.com

PGA West Jack Nicklaus Private Course, Page 175

55-955 PGA Boulevard
La Quinta, CA 92255
(760) 564-7111
www.pgawest.com

PGA West Pete Dye Stadium Course, Page 176
55-955 PGA Boulevard
La Quinta, CA 92255
(760) 564-7111
www.pgawest.com

PGA West Jack Nicklaus Tournament, Page 176
55-955 PGA Boulevard
La Quinta, CA 92255
(760) 564-7111
www.pgawest.com

PGA West Arnold Palmer Course, Page 176
55-955 PGA Boulevard
La Quinta, CA 92255
(760) 564-7111
www.pgawest.com

PGA West Residence Club, Page 177
55-955 PGA Boulevard
La Quinta, CA 92255
(760) 564-7111
www.pgawest.com

PGA West Signature, Page 180
55-955 PGA Boulevard
La Quinta, CA 92255
(760) 564-7111
www.pgawest.com

Portola Country Club, Page 295
42-500 Portola Avenue
Palm Desert, CA 93360
(760)-346-5481

The Quarry, Page 93

One Quarry Lane
La Quinta, CA 92253
(760) 777-1111

Rancho La Quinta Country Club, Page 151
79295 Rancho La Quinta Drive
La Quinta, CA
(760) 777-7792
www.rancholaquinta.com

Rancho Mirage Golf and Tennis, Page 259
38-500 Bob Hope
Rancho Mirage, CA 92270
(760) 324-4711
http://www.ranchomiragegolf.com

The Reserve, Page 76
14001 Reserve Drive
Indian Wells, CA 92210
(760) 568-559
thereserveclub.com

Santa Rosa Cove, Page 116
4991 Eisenhower Drive
La Quinta, CA 92253
(760) 777-7621

Shadow Mountain Resort, Page 227
45750 San Luis Rey Avenue
Palm Desert, CA 92260
(760) 346-6123

Silver Sands Racquet Club, Page 231
74155 Country Club Drive

Palm Desert, CA 92260
(760) 340-1667
http://silversandshoa.com

Spa Villas, Page 143
49-499 Eisenhower Drive
La Quinta, CA 92253
(760) 564-4111
www.laquintaresort.com

Springs, Page 229
One Duke Drive
Rancho Mirage, CA 92270
(760) 324-8292
http://springsclub.com

Stone Ridge, Page 135
34-600 Mission Hills Drive
Rancho Mirage, CA 92270
(760) 324-9400
missionhillssales.com

Sun City Palm Desert, Page 176
38180 Del Webb Blvd
Palm Desert, CA 92211
(760)-200-2100
scpdca.com

Sun City Shadow Hills, Page178
80814 Sun City Boulevard
Indio, CA 92203
(760) 345-4349

Suncrest, Page 180
73-450 Country Club Drive

Palm Desert, CA 92260
(760) 340-2467

Sunrise Country Club, Page 233
71-601 Country Club Drive
Rancho Mirage, CA 92270
(760) 328-6549

Tamarisk Country Club, Page 153
70240 Frank Sinatra Drive
Rancho Mirage, CA 92270
(760) 328-2141

Tennis Villas, Page 144
49-499 Eisenhower Drive
La Quinta, CA 92253
(760) 564-4111
www.laquintaresort.com

Thermal Club, Page 78
86030 62nd Avenue
Thermal, CA 92274
(760)-239-6868

Toscana, Page 74
43-199 Via Lucca
Indian Wells, CA
(760) 404-1444

Thunderbird Country Club, Page 80

70-737 Country Club Drive
Rancho Mirage, CA 92270
(760) 328-2161

The Tradition, Page 82
78505 Old Avenue 52
La Quinta, CA 92253
(760) 563-8723

Trilogy at La Quinta, Page 182
60-151 Trilogy Parkway
La Quinta, CA 92253
(760) 777-6052

Trilogy at the Polo Grounds, Page 184
51682 Hawthorne Court
Indio, CA 92201
(800) 685-6494

Villa Portafino, Page 186
4001 Via Portofino
Palm Desert, CA 92260

Vintage Club, Page 84
75-00l Vintage Drive West
Indian Wells, Ca. 92210
 (760) 340-0500

Westgate, Page 137
34-600 Mission Hills Drive
Rancho Mirage, CA 92270
(760) 324-9400
missionhillssales.com

Woodhaven Country Club, Page 234
41-555 Woodhaven Drive East
Palm Desert, CA 92211
(760) 345-7636
www.woodhavencc.com

Synopses of other John J. Barnes books

and how to buy them.

I've written fiction books you might also enjoy, to include an account of retirees living in a Desert 55+ community similar to those you've been reading about in these pages.

Retirement

One man's adventures exploring life's final frontier

John Barnes

Retirement: One man's adventures exploring life's final frontier was published in 2010 and with zero advertising has sold over 2,000 copies on line at Amazon.com. You'll find it still for sale there.

Synopsis: *A handful of men in their 60's and 70's in Happy Valley, a 55+ gated desert community, deal with adultery, deception, happiness, death, third marriages, sex, singlehood, sickness, success, adult children, failure, friendship, love and loss. If you're young or middle-aged and haven't given much thought to old age, read this book to learn what's in store.*

To purchase *Retirement: One man's adventures exploring life's final frontier* by John. J. Barnes, type the book's name where Amazon.com prompts you on its site. You'll be glad you did.

I've also written short, punchy and highly readable adventure books designed to be read in five hours or less.

Here are the Barry and Rebecca Forester Adventure books by John J. Barnes you can buy on Amazon.com right now:

Available on Amazon.com and Kindle.

DEATH IN SENTARI
A Barry and Rebecca Forester adventure

John J. Barnes

Death in Sentari: A Barry and Rebecca Forester Adventure by John J. Barnes

Synopsis: *When Muslim extremists attack a safari lodge and slaughter Rebecca Jones' parents, she and Barry Forester flee in panic and find haven high in nearby mountains. Pursuers find them, they flee again and journey on bad road across unforgiving African tundra to the capitol. As they near the city, an army general launches an insurrection. Caught in the mayhem, unable to speak the language, to avoid death they kill but soon find themselves imprisoned in the notorious Gulag facing torture and certain death. By then, they've not only fallen in love, they've made questionable life-altering decisions from which there's no turning back.*

Available on Amazon.com and Kindle.

DEATH IN
MONTEVIDEO
A BARRY AND REBECCA
FORESTER ADVENTURE
JOHN J. BARNES

Death in Montevideo: A Barry and Rebecca Forester Adventure by John J. Barnes

Synopsis: *Barry and Rebecca travel to Uruguay at the tip of South America. Their assignment: Stop the illegal sale of software worth millions. Two resourceful enemies stand in their way: sexually voracious female CEO Tama Wu and a heavily muscled psychopath with*

a PhD nicknamed 'The Pole.' The killings begin. Barry gets careless. Rebecca must find him soon or he will die.

Available on Amazon.com and Kindle.

DEATH IN
HAMBURG
A Barry and Rebecca
Forester adventure

John J. Barnes

Death in Hamburg: A Barry and Rebecca
Forester adventure *by John J. Barnes*

Synopsis: *Dragon Motors President Tama Wu
suspects that her archenemy, The Pole, did not die in
Montevideo. She's sparing no expense to learn the truth.
If he's found alive, she'll capture, torture and kill
him. Meanwhile, a young Polish woman sold into sexual
slavery escapes and begins hunting down and killing
those who enslaved her. The killings escalate as a
freighter concealing weapons-grade uranium stolen
from North Korea approaches Hamburg. Barry and
Rebecca get involved. Rebecca is trapped and Barry
must find a way to save her.*

Available on Amazon.com and Kindle.

Death in LA: A Barry and Rebecca Forester adventure *by John J. Barnes*

Synopsis: *Members of the Black Tong, a Chinese American criminal enterprise discover Barry and Rebecca's second home in southern France, causing them to flee to LA, where they stay temporarily with Tama Wu, who's left China to become a Hollywood producer. Tama rescues a young aspiring actress from being raped outside a Malibu mansion and wounds the rapist, who's connected to the Tong. The action switches from LA to Mexico City as Barry and Rebecca desperately seek to find a way to save themselves, Tama and the young girl from Tong assassins who've discovered their location.*

Available on Amazon.com and Kindle.

Allen Island

A Barry and Rebecca Forester adventure

John Barnes

Allen Island: A Barry and Rebecca Forester adventure *by John J. Barnes*

Synopsis: *Evil Russian oligarch Alexi Orloff seizes Rebecca Forester and jails her on his private island off the Kenyan coast, where the brown skins and shaved heads live. There, he conducts a bizarre sexual experiment. In a small arena custom-built for hand-to-hand warfare, he stages battles between those who displease him and ravenous wolves. If Barry does not find Rebecca in time, she'll be thrown to the wolves while Orloff and his henchmen watch. Getting to the island won't be easy. Someone Barry trusts has betrayed him and plans to lead him into a trap.*
Available on Amazon.com and Kindle. *m*

Death in Dubai

Barry and Rebecca Forester's final adventure

John Barnes

Death in Dubai: Barry and Rebecca Foresters'
final adventure by John J. Barnes

Synopsis: *Old friend Tama Wu has become
the target of a vicious scam. Barry and Rebecca take
Ania Urban, a former sex slave and trained killer to
LA to help Tama. Barry and Rebecca's
college-drop-out son Jason arrives. He and Ania hook
up. Russian oligarch Alexi Orloff's shaved headed
thugs kidnap Jason and take him to Dubai. Alexi
Orloff invites Rebecca to join him. If she refuses,
Jason will die. If she goes, she may die instead.*
Available on Amazon.com and Kindle.

John J. "Jamie" Barnes has lived seven years in a southern California desert 55+ community. A graduate of Harvard College (A.B., Economics), he's done business start-ups for AT&T International all over the world. After retirement, he consulted in Eastern Europe for six years, ran a foundation in Poland and did doctoral work in Modern Languages and Critical Theory at Wayne State and Cornell Universities, passing 20 hours of oral and written doctoral exams before moving to San Marino, California without writing a thesis. He speaks French and German badly but reads both languages reasonably well, has served on the volunteer board of the Detroit Institute of Arts Volunteer Board of Directors and Pasadena's Frostig School Board of Directors, is an avid tennis and pickle ball player and now enjoys retirement, which as of January 2016 is entering its 23rd year.